Mary Linskill

**In Exchange for a Soul**

Vol. I

Mary Linskill

**In Exchange for a Soul**
*Vol. I*

ISBN/EAN: 9783337051808

Printed in Europe, USA, Canada, Australia, Japan

Cover: Foto ©ninafisch / pixelio.de

More available books at **www.hansebooks.com**

## A Novel

BY
### MARY LINSKILL

AUTHOR OF
'BETWEEN THE HEATHER AND THE NORTHERN SEA,' 'HAGAR,'
'THE HAVEN UNDER THE HILL,' ETC.

IN THREE VOLUMES
VOL. I.

London
CHATTO AND WINDUS, PICCADILLY
1887

*[The right of translation is reserved]*

### Dedicated

TO

HYACINTHE, LADY DALBY.

# CONTENTS OF VOL. I.

| CHAPTER | | PAGE |
|---|---|---|
| I. | THORHILDA THEYN | 1 |
| II. | A NORTH YORKSHIRE FISHER-MAIDEN | 12 |
| III. | ULVSTAN BIGHT | 24 |
| IV. | SQUIRE THEYN'S SISTER, AND SOME OTHERS | 31 |
| V. | ON THE FORECLIFF | 42 |
| VI. | 'ABOVE THE SOUND OF THE SEA' | 48 |
| VII. | THE RECTORY AT MARKET YARBURGH | 62 |
| VIII. | AT GARLAFF GRANGE | 75 |
| IX. | 'LOVE'S NOBILITY' | 83 |
| X. | 'IN ALL TIME OF OUR WEALTH' | 100 |
| XI. | CONCERNING HAPPINESS | 109 |
| XII. | IN THE VILLAGE STREET | 120 |
| XIII. | EXTENUATING CIRCUMSTANCES | 128 |
| XIV. | THE STORY OF A MISTAKE | 136 |
| XV. | SOME ART CRITICS | 148 |

| CHAPTER | | PAGE |
|---|---|---|
| XVI. BARBARA BETRAYS HERSELF | - | 162 |
| XVII. A REVELATION | - | 173 |
| XVIII. AT ORMSTON MAGNA | - | 188 |
| XIX. UNDER THE LARCHES | - | 203 |
| XX. THE CANON AND HIS NIECE | - | 216 |
| XXI. THAT WAS THE DAY WE LOVED, THE DAY WE MET | - | 222 |
| XXII. IN YARVA WYKE | - | 237 |
| XXIII. CANON GODFREY AND HIS NEPHEW | - | 249 |
| XXIV. 'SWEET THE HELP OF ONE WE HAVE HELPED' | - | 264 |
| XXV. DAMIAN ALDENMEDE AT THE RECTORY | - | 277 |

# IN EXCHANGE FOR A SOUL.

## CHAPTER I.

### THORHILDA THEYN.

'O what a thing is man! how far from power,
    From settled peace and rest!
He is some twenty several men at least
    Each several hour!'
GEORGE HERBERT.

'HAPPY! What *right* hast thou to be happy?'

This pregnant question, asked once emphatically by Carlyle, and repeated often by him in modified form, is certainly worthy of attention. Consciously or unconsciously, the need for happiness is a factor in the life of each one of us: and no attempt to deny the need is so successful as we dream.

Thorhilda Theyn was not greatly given to self-questioning. So far, perhaps, there had seemed to be no special necessity for it in her life—that is, no necessity caused by pressure of outward circumstance, by any of the strong crises that come upon most human lives at one time or another. She was yet young; she was very beautiful. Life was all before her, and the promise of it exceeding fair. What need for question so far?

Yet as she stood there on that blue, breezy May morning, she felt herself decidedly in the grasp of some new spirit of inquiry, born within her apparently of the day and of the hour, strong at its birth, and demanding attention.

The waters of the North Sea were her grand outlook. They were spread all before her across the bay, rippling from point to point, leaping, darting, dancing. The free, fresh, rustling sound was sweeter to her always than the similar sound of the wind in the woodland trees; and it was soothing as soft music to watch the wavelets at play, leaping into light, flashing for a gay, glad moment, then dissolving instantly into apparent nothingness. Over and over it was all repeated, and the entrancingly uncertain certainty was as a spell to hold her there by the foot of the tall cliffs of Ulvstan Bight as one held in a dream.

'They say that life is like that—the poets, the philosophers,' Thorhilda said to herself, leaning lightly upon the parapet, tall and straight, and still, and beautiful. She was dressed as became her stately style, in a fashion that might have been of that day or of this, so few of its details were borrowed from any extraneous source. Her gown fell gracefully about her feet; her long cloak almost covered it; her small hands were crossed lightly, and held her hat, so that the fair face, so sweet and yet so strong, was all unshaded from the morning sun. And it was a face that could well bear the full, clear light; no thought-line was yet graven upon the wide forehead, on either side of which the dark abundant hair was braided 'Madonna-wise'; deep, changeful gray eyes looked out from below the white drooping lids that give to any face a touch of pathos—a touch contradicted at that moment on Thorhilda's face by an evidently half-unconscious smile, which played fitfully about her mouth. It was a mouth that was almost childlike in the fine roundness of its curves, and yet it was the lower part of the face that displayed firmness, decision. The eyes were all gentleness, all tenderness, in repose. When the lips smiled in conversation the eyes smiled too, and a fascinating piquancy of expression would suddenly light up features that had seemed too grave and gentle ever to be piquant. The effect was apt to be surprising; but it was always a pleasant surprise, and betrayed the observer to admiration, though no such effect had been expected on the one side, or certainly intended on the other. Thorhilda was innocent of the art of producing effects. That such an art existed was a matter of hearsay, and therefore dubious.

'They say that life is like that!' she had murmured half audibly, ' like

> ' " A momentary ray,
> Smiling in a winter's day.
> 'Tis a current's rapid stream,
> 'Tis a shadow, 'tis a dream."

So wrote Francis Quarles, over two hundred years ago; so others have written,' she went on. 'And yet how different one feels! I feel this morning as if life were ages long. I have lived but four-and-twenty years, yet I seem to have centuries in my personal memory.'

Presently definite thought passed on into indefinite. Dreams came up out of the past, with reminiscence sad and sunny; and finally came that bright yet questioning mood of which mention has been made already, the disposition to ask herself, not 'What right have I to be happy?' but '*Why* am I so happy?'

Once as she leaned by the edge of the sea-wall, watching the gulls float up and down with folded wing and yielding breast upon the gently heaving waters, an answer came suddenly. Was it from the heart, or from the brain only? Though she was alone, she blushed; the long eyelashes drooped; and a little instant, negative movement of the head might have been detected had anyone to detect it been there.

'No, *no!* It is not that, it is not *that!*' she made haste to assure herself. 'I do not feel that *he* could make happiness of mine. No, it is not that!'

It was perhaps significant that she did not long continue to dwell upon the idea of Percival

Meredith. He was a neighbour, the owner of Ormston Magna, a place some three miles nearer to the sea than Yarburgh; indeed, from its terraced gardens you could look out over the wide expanse of the German Ocean. Percival, who was an elderly-looking man, if you considered his thirty-four summers, lived at Ormston with his mother, a lady who might easily have been mistaken for his elder sister. It had been made evident for some time to Canon and Mrs. Godfrey that the Merediths had especial motives for gladly accepting every invitation that was sent to them from the Rectory, and for inviting the inhabitants of the Rectory to Ormston on any and every possible occasion. Of late Thorhilda had herself discovered the reason of all this; and she was perplexed, pleased, perturbed by turns. Only at rare moments was she conscious of any true satisfaction in thinking of Percival Meredith and his too evident intentions.

Yes; it was certainly significant that at the present moment she made haste to put away all thought of him, and went on thinking, meditating, on the strong, glad sense of her life and its happiness. She was not old enough, or tried enough, to know how on such days the mere sense of living is enough for unusual exultation.

> 'Bliss was it on that morn to be alive,
> But to be young was very heaven.'

So wrote Wordsworth; but he had passed his youth when he wrote this.

Had anyone in Thorhilda's circle of friends —Gertrude Douglas, for instance, who was considered to be her most intimate friend— been asked to give a reason for Miss Theyn's happiness, Gertrude would have made answer,

'How should she not be happy?'

Her home in the house of her uncle, Canon Godfrey, the Rector of Market Yarburgh, was, admittedly, as happy a home as a woman could have. The Canon's wife, Milicent Godfrey, was the sister of Thorhilda's dead mother; and, being a childless woman herself, with a passionate love for children, she had done all that might be done to make Thorhilda's life a life full of all sweetness, all light, all good. It was for her niece's sake that the old Rectory had been refurnished, made beautiful with all artistic beauty that fair means could command.

Indeed, nothing had been left undone that love could suggest as better to be done. And Thorhilda, having a keen appreciation of the material good of life—*too* keen, said some of the friendliest of her friends—was neither unconscious nor ungrateful. Therefore what reason for not being happy?

Is it true, that old saying, 'Every light has its shadow'?

Scientifically, it must be true, always; but surely the analogy will not bear stretching to meet and to fit this human life in every possible phase. We know that it will not, and are happier for the knowledge—happier and better.

But the bright picture of Thorhilda Theyn's life was not without that enhancing touch of depth in the background of it, which gives both to colour and light their rightful prominence and effect. There had been hours, nay days, when that dark background had claimed more of the girl's life than any foreground object that could be put before her for her distraction.

'I must think of these things, Aunt Milicent,' she had said. 'Garlaff Grange is my own home. They are my own people who live there.'

'No; there I *cannot* agree,' Mrs. Godfrey had replied. 'Your mother gave you to me solemnly, prayerfully, when she was dying. She entreated me to promise that the Rectory should be your home. . . . I have tried to keep my promise.'

The touch of emotion with which these and other sayings were uttered was usually conclusive. Thorhilda had no heart to go on with arguments presented to her only by an inadequate sense of duty. If people so much older and wiser than herself as Canon Godfrey and her aunt considered that it was her wisdom to sit still, why should she not agree—especially since movement in the direction indicated by conscience was so eminently distasteful?

And yet from time to time conscience would have its way. Did she really do all that it was her duty to do in going to the Grange now and then when it was quite convenient to her aunt to drive round that way; in sending presents on birthdays and Christmas Days; in calling occasionally to see how her sister Rhoda was, or to inquire after her aunt Averil? It was not pleasant for her to go there—the reverse of that—and she did not for a moment imagine that she gave any pleasure by going. She was saved from all illusion on that head. So far as she could remember, her father had never once in his life said, 'I am glad to see you!'—never, even when she was a child, offered her any greeting or parting kiss. Once or twice he had shaken hands; once or twice he had—not at all ironically—taken off his hat as the Rectory carriage drove away with only Thorhilda in it; and there had seemed nothing incongruous in his doing so.

His daughter knew little of him except what she heard from others; and it was long since she had heard any pleasant thing. For years past everything had been going down at Garlaff Grange, and though repeated efforts had been made by Canon Godfrey and others to stop the descent, no such efforts had availed, and it was long now since Squire Theyn had permitted anything of what he termed 'interference.'

'Ah'll ha' neä mair on't!' he had said to his only son, Hartas, on one occasion.

Canon Godfrey had been spending an hour

with Squire Theyn—spending it mostly in earnest entreaty; and he had left the Grange with the Squire's 'words of high disdain' ringing in his ears painfully.

'Ah'll ha' neä mair on't!' repeated the old man; and Hartas helped greatly to confirm him in this decision.

The younger man's dislike to anything that could touch his liberty was at least as strong as the same feeling in the elder one. There were some who said that Squire Theyn and his son were not unworthy of each other; and it is possible that the saying had more in it than appeared on the surface. Certainly it was one to bear investigation, had any analytically minded person been drawn to interest himself in the matter. And a student bent upon humanity might have travelled far before finding two more unique subjects for his research.

# CHAPTER II.

### A NORTH YORKSHIRE FISHER-MAIDEN.

'She was a careless, fearless girl,
 And made her answer plain,
Outspoken she to earl or churl,
 Kindhearted in the main.'
CHRISTINA ROSSETTI.

WHY Thorhilda's thoughts, as she stood there by the margent of the sea, should suddenly be drawn to her brother Hartas, she could hardly have told in that first moment. She had not been thinking of him as she stood, letting the breezes blow upon her forehead, turning from watching the wide, white-flecked sea to note the fisher folk on the beach and on the quays. She knew nothing of any of these save by hearsay, and yet she was aware of something prompting her interest in a group of tall, handsome fisher-girls who were down by the edge of the tide—such girls as you would hardly see anywhere else in England for strength and straightness, for roundness of form and bright, fresh healthfulness of countenance.

They wore blue flannel petticoats, and rough, dark-blue masculine-looking guernseys of their own knitting. Their heads were either bare, or covered with picturesque hoods of blue cotton—pink, lilac, buff, pale blue. One, the tallest of them, and decidedly the handsomest, had no bonnet at all, and her rich chestnut hair blew about in the breeze in shining rings and curls in a way that attracted Thorhilda's attention, and even her admiration, though as a rule she had slight sympathy with the 'admired disorder' school of æsthetics. And as she watched the girl, all at once there darted a new thought across her brain, a new and disturbing conviction.

'That is Barbara Burdas!' she said to herself. Then she smiled a little, and wondered at the force of a feeling that had so far-off a cause.

Miss Theyn knew very little of Barbara Burdas. Though the reputation of the handsome fisher-girl was rapidly spreading along the coast from Flamborough Head to Hild's Haven, her name had seldom been heard within the walls of the Rectory at Market Yarburgh; but one day Canon Godfrey had spoken in a somewhat grieving tone to his wife concerning some new rumour which had reached his ear—a story in which both Barbara's bravery and the influence of her beauty were brought into prominence. Mrs. Godfrey tried to prevent his sorrow from deepening.

'It will do the girl no harm,' she said, with her usual somewhat emphatic vivacity. 'Barbara Burdas is as good a woman as I am, and as strong. Think of her life, of all she is doing for her grandfather and the children! Oh, a little admiration won't harm Barbara! It may even be some lightness in her life—some relief; I hope it will. She has not known much pleasure.'

Thorhilda being present, Canon Godfrey had made no reply at that moment; but later he had confided to his wife the things that he had heard in the parish concerning Barbara Burdas and her own nephew, Hartas Theyn. Subsequently some guesses had been made by Thorhilda, but they were little more than guesses, arising out of a word dropped by her aunt in an unguarded moment.

Now, seeing Barbara there on the beach, a sudden desire to know something of the truth came upon her; and after a few moments' consideration she left the promenade, and went down between the nursemaids and the babies, the donkeys and the Bath-chairs, to where the shore was wet and shining, and, for the present, almost untrodden. The wind seemed freer, and the sun brighter there by the changing edge of the sea.

Miss Theyn was not a woman to saunter on aimlessly, to wait for an opportunity of speaking to Bab alone. She went straight across the stretch of brown sea-tangle, going directly to the group of laughing girls, with that fine nerve and presence which comes mostly of good health and right training. The laughter died down as she came nearer; and with apparent courtesy Bab and her friends half turned and drew together waitingly. They were not unused to conversation with curious strangers.

Thorhilda was the first to speak. She

looked at Bab as she did so, and there was involuntary admiration in her look, which Bab saw, and did not resent. Yet there was an unconscious touch of scorn about the fisher-girl's mouth, a half-disdain in the inquiring glance she fixed upon the lady whose delicate gray silk dress had come in contact with the slimy weed and the coarse, brown sand, and whose small dainty boots were surely being ruined as they sank and slipped among the great drifting fronds that lay heaped upon the shale. Thorhilda understood the disdain.

'Are you not Barbara Burdas?' she asked, in her clear yet gentle voice, as she drew quite near.

Bab hesitated a moment, during which her lips compressed themselves firmly, yet without discharging the scorn from the curves at the corners. Her gaze was still steady and inquiring. A slight tinge of colour crept under the creamy olive of her cheek.

She was about to reply; but it was a moment too late. Her friend, Nan Tyas, a young fishwife, almost as tall, almost as handsome as herself, but in a different way, had come to an end of her slight store of patience.

Looking over Bab's shoulder, her keen dark eyes glittering as she stared straight into Miss Theyn's face, an expression of suspicion on every feature, she asked:

'Wheä telled ya her neäme?'

This was meant to be facetious, and there was *esprit de corps* enough among the girls to cause it to be received as it was meant. A general titter went round, in the midst of which another voice found courage to remark:

'Mebbe she kenned it of her oän sharpness.'

A second laugh was heard, less restrained than before.

Thorhilda looked on with interest, but not smilingly, still less resentfully. The moment and its experience were new to her. Moreover, she discerned that a grave clear look from Bab was quelling the tendency to sarcasm.

'Haud yer tongues, ya fools,' Bab said quietly, but with a certain force in the tone of her voice.

Then she turned to Miss Theyn, the

lingering displeasure still about her mouth. Speaking with decidedly less of the northern accent and intonation than before, she said:

'Yes, Barbara Burdas; that's what they call ma. Ah'm noän shamed o' my name.... Did ya want anything wi' me?'

'Yes; I wished to speak to you for awhile. I do not know that I have much of importance to say at present; but I wished to know you, to ask you one or two questions. I thought that perhaps your friends would permit me to speak to you alone.'

A certain power in Miss Theyn's glance as she looked round upon the six or seven young women might have as much to do with their compliance as the tone of expectant authority which she involuntarily used. They smiled satirically to each other; and then went gliding away with the strong easy grace of movement which seems their birthright. Thorhilda watched them admiringly for a few moments; then she turned to walk with Bab in the opposite direction; and for a little while there was silence; but it was not at all an awkward silence. Though the moment was not a facile one, the elements of awkwardness did not exist for these two, who walked there side by side, so near, yet so widely separated.

Again it was Thorhilda who spoke first. She did so naturally, and without constraint.

'Thank you for telling me your name,' she said. 'It is only fair that I should tell you mine in return; it is Thorhilda Theyn.'

Bab did not quite stay the firm step that was going on over the beach; but Miss Theyn perceived the partial arresting of movement; she divined the cause of it; and she understood the presence of mind that gave Bab the power to go on again as if nothing had happened.

'Then you'll live at the Grange,' Bab said, speaking as if even curiosity were far from her.

'No,' Thorhilda replied. 'I live at Market Yarburgh, at the Rectory; but the Grange is my real home.'

'An' the Squire is yer father?'

'Yes. . . . And Hartas Theyn is my brother.'

The sun was still shining down with brilliancy upon the blue waters of the North Sea, upon the white wavelets that broke gently but just below where the two girls were sauntering. A couple of sea-gulls were crying softly overhead; the fishing boats in the offing were ploughing their way northward. A light breeze fluttered the loops of grey ribbon that fastened Thorhilda's dress. Bab's attention seemed drawn in rather a marked way to the ribbon. Her eyes followed its fluttering as she walked on in silence, but it was not of the ribbon that she was thinking.

Perhaps she was hardly thinking at all in any true sense of the word; yet she was aware of some new and gentle influence that was stealing upon her swiftly, awakening an admiration that was almost emotion; subduing the natural pride that was in her; the strong natural independence of her spirit, an independence of which she was as utterly unconscious as she was of the ordinary pulsations of her heart; but which was yet one of the dominant traits of her nature; and produced difficulties, perplexities, which she had often found bewildering, but never more bewildering than at the present moment. Here was one, far above her by birth, by beauty, by position, by education, yet possessing a something (Bab did not know it to be sympathy) that had the power to charm, to extract the bitterness from pain, and the sting from an unacknowledged dread. Bab hesitated some time, sighing as she repressed one impulse after another toward unsuitable speech. The right words would not come. At last came some awkward ones.

'If ya've anything to saäy, Miss Theyn, ya'd better say it,' the girl remarked, decidedly more in the tone of one urging blame than deprecating it.

'It is evident that you have nothing to fear,' Thorhilda replied, turning to look into the proud yet winning face so near her own.

'Fear!' exclaimed Bab, a great scorn flashing in her eyes and on her lips. 'Fear! what would *I* ha' to fear, think ya? If ya dream that I'm feared o' yon brother o' yours, or of ony mischief he can bring aboot for me, ya can put away the notion without a second thowt. It's as big a mistake as you've ever made. Fear! I'm moän feared of him. . . . Noä! . . . But Ah know what it is, Miss Theyn. I know what's brought you here: *you're feared for him*—for your brother! You're feared he's goin' to disgrace hisself, an' you, wi' marryin' a flither\*-picker. Don't hev no fear o' that sort, Miss Theyn!' And here even Bab's voice grew fainter as her breathing became overpowered by betraying emotion. 'Don't hev no fear o' that sort. I'll . . . well, I'll let ya know when he's i' daänger!'

It was evident that Bab had not intended to end her speech thus; and other things more important were evident also. Thorhilda's experience had not been wide, but she had her woman's instincts to guide her, and her instinct told her plainly that Bab's emotion could only have one cause. This and other new knowledge complicated the feeling which had brought Miss Theyn to saunter there, in the very middle of Ulvstan Bight, with Barbara Burdas.

Other complications were at hand. Thorhilda herself hardly knew what drew her to notice that Bab's perturbation had suddenly and greatly increased, but instantly her eyes followed the direction of her companion's eyes,

---

\* Flithers = limpets, used for bait.

and almost to her distress she saw that the figure advancing rapidly toward them over the beach was the figure of her brother Hartas. Thorhilda's exclamation of concern did not escape Bab's notice.

# CHAPTER III.

### ULVSTAN BIGHT.

'For hast thou not a herald on my cheek,
 To tell the coming nearer of thy ways,
   And in my veins a stronger blood that flows,
 A bell that strikes on pulses of my heart,
   Submissive life that proudly comes and goes
 Through eyes that burn, and speechless lips that part?
   And hast thou not a hidden life in mine,
   In thee a soul which none may know for thine?'
                           MARK ANDRÉ RAFFALOVITCH.

HARTAS THEYN was coming down the beach slowly, yet with more intentness in his deliberate gait than was usually to be observed. He had seen from the road by the Forecliff that the lady who was walking with Barbara Burdas was none other than his elder sister.

Thorhilda consciously repressed all outward sign as she watched his approach; her face did not betray the sadness she felt as she noted his slouching air—his shabby, shapeless clothing. The very hat he wore, an old gray felt, seemed to betray what manner of man its wearer had come to be; and as he came nearer, his hands in the pockets of his trousers, a pipe between his lips, a sullen, defiant, yet questioning look in the depths of his dark eyes, a touch of something that was almost dread entered into her feeling. It was but momentary, this strange emotion; and she offered her greeting without more restraint than was usual between them.

'You did not expect to see me here, Hartas?' she said pleasantly.

'No, I didn't,' replied the young man, after half a minute's irritating silence. 'An' if I'm to tell the truth, I don't know 'at I'd any particular wish to see you.'

And his eyes flashed a little, as if conscious of a certain amount of daring in his speech.

If this daring were ventured upon for Bab's sake, or because of her presence there, it was a mistake; but this Hartas had not discernment enough to perceive. Bab was looking on with interest, but she repressed all tendency to smile.

Thorhilda replied instantly and easily:

'That is not polite, Hartas,' she said. 'But let it pass. I did not come here to irritate you. And——'

'Could you say what you did come for?' interrupted Hartas, with a certain coarse sharpness in his tone.

'Readily. I came down to make the acquaintance of Barbara Burdas. I wished to know her; I had wished it for some time. So far, I am glad I did come. Don't try to make me regret it.'

'I don't spend my breath in such efforts as them, as a rule,' rejoined the young man, taking his pipe from his mouth, and speaking with evident strong effort to restrain himself. 'But have a care! I don't force myself upon *your* friends.'

'True,' said Thorhilda; and again, before she could find the word she wished to use, the opportunity was taken from her.

'D'ya want yer sister to think she's forced herself upon a friend o' yours?' Bab asked, still seeming as if she tried to restrain the sarcastic smile that appeared to play about her lips almost ceaselessly. Hartas Theyn's manner changed instantly in replying to Bab. It was as if the better nature within him asserted itself all at once; his higher manhood responded to her slightest touch.

'I don't want no quarrellin',' he replied, speaking with a mildness and softness so new in him that even his sister discerned it with an infinite surprise. 'I don't want no quarrellin', an' it's only fair to expect that if I keep away fra *them*, as I always hev done' [this with an unmitigated scorn], 'they'll hev the goodness to keep away fra me. Friends o' *that sort* 's best separated; so I've heard tell afore to-day.'

Then, warming with his own eloquence, Hartas turned again to Thorhilda, saying emphatically:

'I mean no harm; an' as I said just now, I want no quarrellin'; but if you want to keep out o' mischief, keep away fra me; an' from all interference in my affairs. I can manage them for myself, thank ya all the same.'

Thorilda hesitated a moment, recognising the effort Hartas had made, and also the element of fairness in his words, yet it was inevitable that other thoughts should force themselves upon her.

'Hartas, do you remember that you are my brother?' she asked after a moment of swift, deep thinking.

'An' what o' that? It's neither your fault nor mine.'

'No; it is no one's fault; but it is a fact, a fact that means much, and, for me, involves much. If I could forget it I should be—well, something I hope I am not. Fortunately for me I cannot forget it; more fortunately still, I cannot altogether ignore it. I cannot let you and your life's deepest affairs pass by me as if no tie existed. . . . I do not wish to forget or to ignore. Why should you wish it?'

'Because I'm made of a different sort o' stuff—a commoner sort, if you will; an' because I'm cast in a different mould. Say what you like, it isn't easy for you to look down—fool as I am I can see as much as that. But, *take my word for it, it isn't any easier for me to look up.* An' why should either you or me strive to look up or down against the grain? Because the world expects it! Then let it expect. I'm good at disappointin' expectations o' that sort. We're better apart, *an' you know it!*' Then turning away, a little excited, a little angry, perturbed by nervous perturbations of various kinds, he lifted his eyes to discern the approach of influences yet more disturbing to him than any he had encountered that luckless morning. And yet it was only two ladies who were approaching, two elderly and, more or less, elegantly dressed ladies. Hartas instantly divined that they were his aunts in search of Thorhilda.

'Heaven help us!' he exclaimed. 'Here's two more of 'em! Bab, let's fly. There's the cave!'

'*Me* fly!' Bab exclaimed indignantly. 'It will be the first time!' And as she stood watching the two ladies advancing slowly over the slimy, slippery stones and tangle, again the half-satirical smile gathered about her mouth. Hartas watched her face with admiration expressed on every feature of his own; and Thorhilda stood, controlling the fear of a scene that was mingled with her expectancy. Mrs. Godfrey, the Canon's stately and still beautiful wife; Mrs. Kerne, the sister of Squire Hartas, an elderly and rugged-featured woman, the widow of a rich shipowner, had not much in common; and therefore, very wisely, seldom sought each other's society. There certainly seemed to be something strange in the fact of their leaving the wide sea-wall together, and coming down over the wet unstable beach. Besides, there was that in the expression of one of them that was at least ominous.

# CHAPTER IV.

### SQUIRE THEYN'S SISTER, AND SOME OTHERS.

> 'O how this spring of love resembleth
> The uncertain glory of an April day;
> Which now shows all the beauty of the sun
> And by-and-by a cloud takes all away.'
>
> SHAKESPEARE.

'THINK again, Bab!' Hartas whispered to the only quite self-possessed one of the waiting three. 'Think again! There's the Pirates Hole!'

'Go into it, if you're frightened,' replied Bab curtly.

Hartas was silenced; but the unpleasant anticipation of the moment was not done away. He smoked on more vigorously than before. Thorhilda uttered some small nothing to Bab, and then turned to meet the two approaching figures. To her comfort her Aunt Milicent's face was the face it usually was—beautiful, kind, smiling; free from all disfigurement of untoward expression. She was not a woman to mar any influence she might have by uncontrolled feminine petulance.

'Well!' she said cheerfully to Thorhilda. 'I thought you were to wait for me on the promenade, dear! But how lovely this is! How breezy!—And there is Hartas! I haven't seen him for an age. . . . Hartas—how do you do? And how are you all at the Grange? We were thinking of driving round that way, but now we needn't. . . . All quite well? Delightful! But, of course, that doesn't include your poor Aunt Averil. How I should like to hear for once that she was quite well.'

So Mrs. Godfrey ran on in her easy, woman-of-the-world way; glancing at Barbara Burdas, understanding, feeling acutely, all the incongruity of the elements that made up the surrounding atmosphere; knowing herself to be ten times less distressed than Mrs. Kerne, who stood by her side, yet not too near— silent, hard, stern, disapproving to the uttermost. And yet Mrs. Godfrey's social nerves should surely have been as keenly sensitive as those of Squire Theyn's sister. All the world knew of the upbringing of the latter in a household where a fox-hunting mother had been the only feminine influence; and a seldom sober squire, with his like-minded brother, the ruling masculine powers. There had only been one son, the present Squire Theyn; and only one daughter, the present Mrs. Kerne; who had attained the height of her ambition in marrying a rich and vulgar man. The rich man was dead; his widow was a rich woman; and none the more pleasing because during a dozen years of companionship she had managed to add some of her husband's coarsenesses and vulgarities to her own innate ones. The force of natural assimilation was never more clearly proved.

Mrs. Godfrey's early recollections were of a different order. She was one of the five daughters of the Rector of Luneworth, a small village in a midland county—a village where a kindly duke and duchess had reigned supreme, making much of the Rector's pretty children, and affording them many advantages as they grew up which could not otherwise have been obtained. As all the neighbourhood knew, the Miss Chalgroves had shared the lessons that masters came down from London to give to the Ladies Haddingley. And, later in life, some of the Rector's daughters had made a first social appearance on the same evening, and in the same place, as some of their more favoured friends. And they were truly friends, who had remained friendly — much to Milicent Godfrey's permanent good, pleasure, and satisfaction — much to her sister Averil's deterioration. Averil had been the eldest of them all — a clever, fretful, nervous woman, who had all her life magnified her slight ailments into illnesses, and who had condescended to share her sister Grace's home when the latter married Squire Theyn, with an inexpressible disgust. That her sister Milicent had never offered her a couple of rooms at the Rectory at Market Yarburgh remained a standing cause for bitterness. It was not likely to be removed so long as Mrs. Godfrey should care for her husband's peace of mind.

It was the quick sight of Mrs. Kerne, the Squire's widowed sister, that had discerned the group upon the beach. She had met Mrs. Godfrey at the turn leading down to the promenade, accepted her invitation to walk with her to meet Thorhilda with an indifference that was more than merely ungraciousness, and when they found that Thorhilda had left the promenade, her instinct led her to express her shallow satisfaction in somewhat irritating speech. Peering round above the rim of her gold eye-glass, she exclaimed at last:

'There is Miss Theyn!—there is *your niece!*'—speaking as if she herself were no relation whatever. 'What can have led her to seek the society of fish-wives, I wonder? . . . Ah, I see! Master Hartas is there. That accounts. But I did not know that the brother and sister were on such affectionate terms as to induce her to lend her distinguished countenance to such as Bab Burdas for *his* sake. Dear me! What a new departure!'

Mrs. Kerne was a short, stout woman, moving with the ungainly movement natural to her age and proportions. Her red face grew redder as she descended the narrow, unsavoury road that led to the beach, and her usually unamiable expression did not grow more amiable. By the time she had arrived at the point when it was necessary to shake hands with Thorhilda she had—perhaps unaware, poor woman!—acquired a most forbidding aspect. Thorhilda shrank, as from a coming blow; but this was only for a second, her larger nature conquered, and she stood considerate, courageous.

The influence of Barbara Burdas alone held Hartas Theyn to the spot of wet, weed-strewn sand on which he stood, his pipe still in his mouth, his big, unkept brown hands still in the pockets of his trousers. The mere sight of him seemed to awaken the ire of Mrs. Kerne. That he should stand there before her, calmly smoking, with Barbara Burdas by his side, was too much for the small amount of equanimity at her disposal. No description made by means of pen or pencil could do justice to the expression of her face as she broke the brief silence, sniffing the air as she did so as an ill-tempered horse sniffs it at the beginning of the mischief he has it in his head to bring about.

'I can't say that I see exactly why I've been brought down here,' she remarked, glancing from her niece to her even less favoured nephew. 'What is the meaning of it? An' why are you standing there, Hartas, looking more like a fool than usual, if that's possible? . . . I suppose the truth is I've been tricked! brought down here to be introduced to your——'

'Stop a minute,' Hartas interposed, at last taking the pipe from between his lips, putting it behind him, and letting his dark eyes flash their fullest power upon Mrs. Kerne. 'Stop a minute,' he said. 'If you've been brought down here, it's been by no will o' mine. I haven't seen you this year past, and wouldn't ha' minded if I hadn't seen you for years to come. . . . All the same, say what you've got to say to me, but take my advice for once, leave other folks alone—especially folks 'at's never me'lled wi' you.'

'It isn't much I've got to say to you,' Mrs. Kerne replied, the angry colour deepening on her face as she spoke, and a keen light darting from her small eyes. 'It isn't much I've got to say; an' first I may as well just thank you for your plain speaking. I'll not forget it! You may have cause to remember it yourself, sooner or later. It'll not be the first time 'at the readiness of your tongue has had to do with the emptiness of your pocket.'

'Mebbe not,' interrupted Hartas. 'I'd as soon my pockets were empty as try to fill 'em wi' toadyin' rich relations .... Most things has their price.'

'I'm glad you've found that out,' replied Mrs. Kerne. 'But you've more to learn yet, if all be true 'at one hears an' sees. However, as you say, perhaps I'd better leave you to go to ruin by your own road. You've been travellin' on it a good bit now, by all accounts, an' from the very first I've felt that tryin' to stop you would be like tryin' to stop a thunderbolt.'

'Just like that; an' about as much of a mistake,' said Hartas, with an irritating attempt to seem cool. But the effort was obvious, and Thorhilda, who discerned all too plainly whither these amenities were likely to lead, turning to her brother, said gently:

'Hartas, it is my fault that this has happened. I couldn't foresee it, of course. But let us put an end to it. Aunt Katherine will take cold if she remains here on the wet beach any longer; and we are going home—Aunt Milicent and myself. Hadn't you better go too? And shall you be at the Grange to-morrow, in the afternoon? I want to see you. Don't refuse me, Hartas; I don't often ask favours of you.'

It was strange how Thorhilda's voice, speaking gently, kindly, quietly, seemed to change the elements of that untoward atmosphere. Mrs. Kerne's countenance relaxed all unconsciously; Mrs. Godfrey smiled, and turned with a pleasant word to Barbara Burdas, who had been standing there during those brief moments, silent, wondering, perplexed, and not a little saddened. Bab knew nothing of Tennyson, but the spirit of one of the poet's verses was rankling in her heart—

'If this be high, what is it to be low?'

Bab could not put the inquiry in these words, but in her own way, and of her own self, she asked the question; and later, in her own home, it came back upon her with fuller force than ever. Was this the surrounding of the man who had seemed to step down from some higher place, to condescend in speaking to her, to seem as if he stood on the verge of ruin in making known to her his deep and passionate affection? Bab understood much, more even than she knew that she understood, but naturally, from her social standpoint, there was a good deal that was confusing to her. Hitherto she had not cared to know of any dividing lines there might be in ranks above her own, and though discernment had seldom failed her in such cases of pretension as she had come across, she yet had no knowledge of the great gulfs that are fixed between class and class, and are only now and then bridged over by bridges of gold. But ignorant as she might be, she had yet discerned, instantly and instinctively, that Mrs. Godfrey and Miss Theyn were at least as far above Hartas as Hartas was above herself, and that the lines on which Mrs. Kerne's life was laid down were more familiar to him, and, in a certain sense, more consonant, than the lines of the two other lives into which Bab had had so mere a glimpse. Yet brief as the insight had been, it had developed an infinitude of suggestive ideas ; and it was significant that Bab's thought was drawn to dwell mainly upon the gentler, the higher phase of the humanity presented to her in those few moments. Naturally, her thinking and wondering was of a vague and inexact order, but it was not without its influence, for she recognised clearly that the hour of her meeting with Miss Theyn was the most striking landmark of her hitherto uneventful history.

## CHAPTER V.

### ON THE FORECLIFF.

'Whither away, Delight?
  Thou camest but now; wilt thou so soon depart,
 And give me up to-night?
 For weeks of lingering pain and smart,
 But one half-hour of comfort for my heart!'
                              GEORGE HERBERT.

'YES; I'm glad to have seen them,' Bab said to herself, as she stood alone at the door of her grandfather's cottage at night.

The children were all in bed, little Stevie with his grandfather, Jack and Zeb in another bed in the far corner of the attic. Ailsie was in Bab's room, down below, a little square, dark place, with only room for a bed and a chair and the box in which Bab kept her 'Sunday things'—her own and Ailsie's, and the latter were more than the former. Few things pleased Bab more than to be able to buy some bit of bright ribbon for Ailsie's hat, or a kerchief for Ailsie's neck. No child on the Forecliff was more warmly and prettily clad than Ailsie Burdas.

It was moonlight now, the tide was half high, and the bay was filled from point to point with the sparkling of the silent silver sea. There were a few fishing-cobles in the offing, two or three more were landing, making a picturesque group of dark, moving outlines upon the white margin of the waters. Bab was no artist, no poet, but something of the poet temperament there was in the girl, and that something was heightened at the present moment by the emotion she was contending against, striving to hide its intensity even from her own self. Bab had never acknowledged, even in her inmost thought, that there was any possibility of Hartas Theyn winning from her a return of the affection he professed so passionately. Rather was she conscious of that spirit of rebellion which so often dawns with a dawning love, the spirit of fear, of shrinking reluctance.

Hitherto the thought of becoming the wife of a man whose position in life was superior to her own had held but little temptation for her. She was not dazzled by the knowledge of Hartas Theyn's higher standing, of his better birth, of his reputed wealth. She would have been glad to exchange her life for one that offered greater freedom from care, greater ease, more ability to procure for herself and those belonging to her some of the things that were now counted as luxuries not to be thought of; but she had never been prepared to sacrifice herself too completely for such advantages as these. She was young and strong, and as willing to work as she was able. Why, then, should she dream of purchasing at a great price the things she did not very greatly desire to have?

But now to-night other thoughts came across her as she stood there, other visions filled her brain, vague visions of a gentler and more beautiful life—a life far from all roughness and rudeness—in a word, the life that might be lived by the woman to whom Miss Theyn would say, 'My sister!'

'*My sister!*' Bab had said the words to herself; then she uttered them half-audibly, with a thrill like that of the lover who first says to himself, 'My wife.'

Could Thorhilda Theyn have known it all, could she have looked but one moment into Bab's heart and brain as the girl stood there by the cottage door, feeling almost as if her very breathing were restrained by the force of the new vision, the compelling touch of the new affection, surely for very humility Miss Theyn would have been sad at heart. It was well for her peace that she might not know.

Bab had never before come into contact with any woman of such winning grace, such refined loveliness; never before had she been moved by such attractive gentleness. And there was something more than these — a mystic and far-off something that drew the untrained fisher-girl with a strong and strange fascination, a fascination that she could neither understand nor resist.

'I'd lay my life down for her,' she said, blushing as she spoke for the warmth of her own word, though no one was by to hear it, or to hold her in contempt for evermore for having used it. The blush was the sign of her heart's inexperience.

Thinking thus of Miss Theyn, it was not wonderful that softened thoughts of Miss

Theyn's brother should come; that his humility of manner to herself should appear in a new and more attractive light; that the remembrance of his affection should have more force to touch her own; that his oft-repeated assurance of life-long protection and unfailing devotion should appeal more strongly to her imagination. Ah, what a dream it was! how bright! how sweet! how possible! but, alas, how very brief!

Bab would not look at the ending of the dream: she put it away resolutely. Some day she would be compelled to look at it, but not to-night, not to-night. It was as if she herself were pleading with herself for a little good, a little beauty, a little softness, a little ease. Some day she might have to pay the price for the dream. Well, let the demand be made, and she would honour it— for Miss Theyn's sake she would honour it, though it cost all that she had, to the last limit.

'Yes, I'd do that; I'd lay down my life if so 'twere to be that she needed it!' Bab repeated, still standing there, watching the dark, picturesque grouping of the men and boats upon the silver of the beach, the swiftly-changing lights and shadows seeming to correspond with the changes of her own thought and emotion.

Presently a voice broke upon the silence, not roughly or rudely, yet with a strangely jarring effect upon her present mood, an effect that was for the instant almost as the first rising of anger. No intrusion could have been more unwelcome.

## CHAPTER VI.

### 'ABOVE THE SOUND OF THE SEA.'

'" Jessie, Jessie Cameron,
   Hear me but this once," quoth he.
" Good luck go with you, neighbour's son,
   But I'm no mate for you," quoth she.
Day was verging toward the night,
   There beside the moaning sea,
Dimness overtook the light,
   There where the breakers be.
" O Jessie, Jessie Cameron,
   I have loved you long and true."
" Good luck go with you, neighbour's son,
   But I'm no mate for you."'
CHRISTINA ROSSETTI.

THE voice was the voice of David Andoe, the brother of Nan Tyas, a brave, strong, young fisherman, with that slow solemnity of speech and movement which seems always to have been won out of the moments of strife with death and danger. David was not surprised to find Bab standing there, though it was nearly midnight and the world about her was all asleep. Like others of his craft, he was used to the keeping of untimely hours.

No, he had no surprise; but an unusual sense of satisfaction came upon him, almost overpowering him for the moment.

'Waitin' for daäylight, Bab?' he asked stopping near the door of the cottage and resting upon the ground the end of an oar which he was carrying homeward for repairs. It looked like a lance as it stood edgewise in the moonlight; and he who carried it might certainly have passed for a young knight of an older time had his dress been other than the knitted blue guernsey and the slouching sou'wester of the north coast. There was little difference between Bab's guernsey and his own; his was knitted in a pattern of broad stripes, hers in a fine 'honey-comb'—the shape was the same precisely.

Bab replied to his question with discouraging carelessness.

'No,' she said; 'I'll get a good sleep in yet afore the sun's above the sea. I'm bound to be at the flither-beds afore five o'clock. . . .

What hev ya got this tide? Not much to boast about, Ah reckon.'

'No,' David replied, half sadly. 'It strikes me 'at it'll be a good while afore anybody hereabouts has aught to boast on again. If you could put a stop to the trawlers to-night, it 'ud take years to fill the sea as full o' fish as it was afore them devil's instriments was invented.'

'The devil has nought to do wi' them,' said Bab, perhaps taking a wider outlook for contradiction's sake. 'There's more i' the heavens above, and i' the e'th beneath, an' i' the waters under the e'th, than such as you an' me knows on. . . . Let 'em be wi' their trawlers, an' their steam fishin' yawls, an' all the rest of it. D'ya think they can alter the ways of Providence? Let 'em be!'

David was silenced for a moment, not feeling quite sure in his own mind that this hopeful philosophy was being countenanced by actual circumstance. Yet for him, as for Bab, there would have been immense, almost insuperable difficulty in trying to set aside, or ignore, the old, tried belief in the wisdom of the ways of Providence. In this they were happy, in having been trained from childhood to at least reverence for a creed that held the Fatherhood of God, the Brotherhood of Christ, as facts that none might disbelieve save to his soul's imperilling. Though no intimate spiritual influence had yet been theirs to draw them to attempt any spiritual life of their own, they were yet aware that such a life might be lived; and David's inner experience had not been so colourless as some of his more fervid mates imagined.

But, like most of his class, he was not given to wear his heart upon his sleeve.

His life, generally, had much in it of which the little world about him was only very dimly aware. He was one of a rather large family. The father was not a sober man; the mother was an ill-tempered woman, dirty withal, and intolerably selfish; caring nothing for the comfort or well-being of her family so that she might sit the long day through upon the doorstep of her cottage, idle, half-clad, and almost repulsive in her personal untidiness. Yet is it strange to confess that David could never rid himself of the old affection for her, the old yearning for her that had so beset him when he was a little lad, suffering keenly from her cruel humours, yet suffering silently and always forgivingly? He had loved his mother and worked for her, and taken thought for her when there was no one else; but he knew that his mother loved not him.

Then naturally, almost inevitably, the affectionateness of his whole strong affectionate nature had gathered itself together in another love—a deeper and more yearning and more passionate love; but, so far, this had seemed to give no sign, save in the keen and ceaseless aching of his heart. No lonely woman ever suffered a lonelier life, or was ever more sensitive to the lightest touch of alleviation.

At the present moment not even Bab herself knew the tremulous way in which one instinct was fighting against another within him.

'Go home now; leave this pre-occupied and unimpressionable girl till a more favourable moment.' So spoke the instinct of common sense. But another and a stronger instinct was there—too strong to utter itself in words. It was by the depth of its silence that he was influenced; and he made a mistake, and he stayed.

'It's all very well to talk i' that way, Bab,' he said at last, answering her word as if no other thought had intervened. 'But when one thinks o' what Ulvstan Bight was nobbut twenty years agone, an' what it is now, one can't but feel half-maddened. Why there isn't a fifth part o' the fish browt into the bay 'at used to be browt in. *It isn't there to be catched;* how can it, wi' the spawn lyin' killed at the bottom o' the sea, mashed wi' the trawl-beam as completely as a railway train 'ud mash a basket of eggs?'

'They tell me, them 'at knows, 'at the spawn doesn't lie at the sea-bottom. It floats on the top.'

'That's true of a few sorts,' said David, half-glad that the girl should reply to him at all; yet suspecting an allusion to one whom he hated with a hate proportionate to his love for Bab. 'It's true of a few sorts; but it isn't true o' the sorts we depend upon for a livin'. I've had proof anuff o' that; an' so hes my father. Why, he was sayin' nobbut yesterday 'at he'd browt into Ulvstan as many as thirteen hundred big fish at a single catch. But he'll never do it again—no, nor no other man.'

'The last season warn't such a bad season for herrin's,' said Bab, still speaking in a conciliatory, but only half-interested way. David Andoe was roused even more than before.

'Herrin's!' he exclaimed. 'There's nowt like the number catched nowadays 'at used to be. Why, I've known mysel' a single boat te take eighteen lasts at a catch; an' sell 'em for ten pound a last.* An' 'twas a reg'lar thing wiv us, when Ah was a lad, te fetch in four or five lasts of a mornin'. Now you may go till you're grey-headed, an' you'll not do it. An'' (here David's voice changed and softened, and betrayed him to his own great pain), ' an' it's noän 'at Ah care so much for money, Bab, nut on my oän account. Thou knows that! Thou knows well anuff why Ah'd be fain to see things as they once was, when every man 'at chose to work could live by his work, whether on land or sea. Ah'm naught at landwork mysel', nut havin' been bred to it; or Ah'd soon try an' see whether Ah couldn't mak' better addlins nor Ah can noo. . . . An'

---

\* A last consists of ten thousand herrings; but a hundred and twenty-four is counted to each hundred. At Yarmouth they count (or used to do so) one hundred and thirty-two.

it's that keeps ma back; an' hinders ma fra speakin' when my heart's achin te saäy a word.'

'Then *don't* say it, David!' protested Bab eagerly; and the tone of her voice attested to the uttermost her sincerity of appeal.

'I *mun* saäy it,' David replied passionately. 'Tho' Ah can't bard the notion o' askin' thee to leave thy gran'father's home, wi' never another home ready for thee to go to. But I'd try to make one ready, Bab; I'd try all I could to make thee a better one! For it breaks my heart to see thee workin' an' toilin' like ony slave. Ay, it *is* bad to bear, when Ah'd work mysel' te skin an' bone te save thee. But what can Ah do when neet after neet we toil an' moil, an' come back i' the mornin' wi' barely anuff te pay for the oil i' the lamp, let alone for the bait, or the wear an' tear o' the lines an' nets? What can Ah do? An' all the while me fearin' 'at somebody else—an' that somebody none so worthy —'ll step in, an' spoil my life for me. . . . Bab, doesn't thee care for me a little? An' me sa troubled wi' carin' for thee! It takes the life out o' me; because there's nought else, no, nought nowheres. An' what is the good o' life to a man if there's noän to care so as how he lives it? Noän to see whether the misery on it's more nor he can bear; noän to help him i' the bearin'; noän to say "Well done!" when he's got the victory; an' noän to speak a word o' comfort when he falls to the ground? What's the good o' life when one hes te live it like that?'

'You might as well say, "What's the good o' life at all?" if ya put it so,' Bab replied, sadly and gravely. The visions of the past half-hour had not been all illumined by the sun.

'I hope I'd never be bold enough i' wickedness to saäy *that!'* David replied. 'Still, it's often been forced in upon me 'at if folks miss the happiness o' life at the beginning they don't easily o'ertake it after. Ah don't know 'at Ah'm so keen set o' hevin' a happy life; still—Ah may say it to thee, Bab—*Ah'm doled o' misery*, the misery 'at sits at a man's fireside, an' dulls the lowe o' the coal, an' taints the tast ov his every bite and sup, no matter how good it be! Eh, but Ah *am* doled o' misery o' that sort, Bab; an' o' some other sorts.

Thee doesn't know the wretchedness of havin' every word — the gentlest ya can utter, replied to wiv a snap o' the tongue, an' a toss o' the head, an' a rasp o' the voice 'at silences ya like a blow frev a hammer, an' makes the heart i' yer body sink as if a stone had been dropped te the middle on't; an' all the while the soul within ya achin', an' achin', an' achin' for the sound of a kindly word till ya're fit te lay doon yer life wi' the longin'. An' it's not for so many days an' weeks ya ha' to bear it—no, nor not for so many months an' years—*it's yer life 'at's goin'*. . . . But, eh, me, what am Ah saying? . . . Thou knows nought o' life o' *that* kind, Bab, an' thou shall never know, so it be that Ah hev my waüy. It all depends on thysel'! . . . Doesn't thee care for me a little, nobbut a little, just anuff to lead thee to promise me to wait a bit? Things'll be better by-an'-by; and there'll be two on us to fight instead o' only thyself. Can't thee saüy a word?'

Bab had listened quite silently; but not without strongly-repressed emotion. The emotion evident in David Andoe had alone been sufficient to awaken her own; and there was more behind. Bab's first girlish thought of love and marriage had been bound up with the thought of David. Many a morning he had helped her to fill her flither-basket out on the rocks at the foot of Yarva-Ness; many a time he had helped her to bring up the lines from her grandfather's boat, or rather the boat in which her grandfather had a single share; many a time he had helped to shorten her daily task of mussel-scaling. Of late Bab had not accepted his help, but this had not greatly distressed him. The meaning of her refusal might not be so untoward as, on the surface of it, it seemed to be. And Bab quite understood. Long ago she had discerned the patience in the man, his faithfulness, his power of loving and suffering in silence; and long ago, at least it seemed long to her now, she had desired to say something that should relieve her own soul from the burden of seeming to encourage attentions she might never accept as they were meant to be accepted.

She knew now that it was not love that was in her heart when she thought of David Andoe, and by consequence his love for her was as a weight that she was fain to put away. Here at last was an opportunity.

'Can't thee say a word, Bab?' David had pled in the gentle, humble tones of true lovingness.

'I'm feared I've nought to say 'at you'd care to hear,' Bab replied quietly, and as she spoke a light, yet chill breeze came up from the sea, making a stir that seemed to cover a little the nakedness of speech. 'I'm noän thinkin' o' changin'! nut i' noä waäy. I'd never leave the childer, still less could I leave my gran'father. Noä, I'll never change.'

'Ah'd niver ask thee to change,' David made haste to reply. 'Ah've thowt it all oot lang sen; an' Ah can see no reason why we shouldn't take a place—a bit bigger nor this—such a one as Storrs' 'ud do right well. An' we'd all live together; an' the most o' the work 'ud fall on me, an' Ah'd be as happy as the day's long. An' surely there'll be a chaänge by-an'-by,' the poor fellow urged, half-forgetful of the prophecy he had uttered but five minutes before. 'Either the fish 'll be easier to come by, or the prices 'll be better, or something 'll turn up i' some way. An' even supposin' noä great chaiinge comes at all, why we'd go on easier together nor apart. There's nought Ah wouldn't do for thee, Bab—noä, nought i' the world. Ah think, indeed, Ah do think, truly, 'at Ah could never live without thee!'

'Don't talk i' that way, David,' she replied. 'An' try an' forget ivery word 'at you've said. There's half-a-dozen lasses an' more i' Ulvstan Bight as 'd be proud an' glad to know 'at you cared for 'em. An' there's good women among 'em; more nor one 'at would make a better wife nor ever I could do wi' four bairns an' a gran'father to start wi'. No, don't saäy no more, David! It 'ud be noä use. Don't saäy no more!'

But David was hurt, and his hurt would have words.

'Ah'll only say this,' he urged, his dark eyes flashing in the moonlight, 'Ah'll only say this—you can't lissen to me, because you've thought of another i' yer mind—another 'at 'll bring ya to misery as sure as you're born; an' make you bite the dust o' the e'th as you've niver been brought to bite it yet. There is a good bit o' pride in ya, Bab—pride 'at Ah've been proud to see, because it seemed to speak o' the high natur 'at was in ya—a natur 'at would never let ya utter no mean word, nor do no mean thing. But yer pride 'll be brought low, *an' he'll do it!* Mark my word. Ah've got no other word to say.'

David Andoe turned away, stung, pained beyond endurance. There had been a certain studied impassiveness in Bab's manner, a cold discouragement that had never been there before for him. He knew nothing of the events of the day, nothing of the new elements that had come into Bab's atmosphere; but he felt the presence of change, and knew it to be full of all adverseness so far as he was concerned. The night was a sleepless one, and tinctured deeply with the one great trial of his much-tried life.

## CHAPTER VII.

### THE RECTORY AT MARKET YARBURGH.

> 'I come from haunts of coot and hern,
>   I make a sudden sally,
> And sparkle out among the fern,
>   To bicker down a valley.
>     ○    ○    ○    ○
> I steal by lawns and grassy plots,
>   I slide by hazel covers;
> I move the sweet forget-me-nots
>   That grow for happy lovers.'
>
> TENNYSON.

THE river Yarva ceases to bicker before it comes to the old town of Market Yarburgh. It winds slowly along between banks so steep as to be almost cliff-like; yet it has four miles farther to flow before reaching the more rugged cliffs by the sea. The ruin of the ancient Priory stands on a rock at least two hundred feet above the river level; and the bridge which unites the divided town has a somewhat perilous look, seeming slender for its great height and length; but since it has stood the traffic of more prosperous times it is probably equal to anything likely to be demanded of it in the present. For Market Yarburgh has pre-eminently the air of a town that has 'seen better days.'

There are quaint coaching inns in the ancient streets; stately-looking old houses of brick and stone stand in high-walled gardens —gardens sloping to the sun for the most part. But indeed everything stands on a slope in Market Yarburgh. The streets, one and all, whether on the east side or on the west, rise at an angle of about forty-five degrees; one and all are narrow; one and all are quiet, clean, silent. Women sit on the doorsteps in the main street, with their knitting in their hands, their children about them, just as they would do in the remotest country village. Fowls peck about among the worn, rounded flint-stones; linen is stretched out across the street to dry. All is slow, dull, primitive, and prosaic.

The Rectory, a long, low, red-brick building, without one trace of architectural beauty natural to it, stood on the hill-top opposite to the ruined Priory. The gardens about it were wide and beautiful, the orchards wide and bountiful. A large fish-pond divided the two; rustic arbours, ancient and modern, were dotted about the grounds everywhere, with garden chairs and tables under drooping trees, placed always where you could have some glimpse of the blue distant beauty of the landscape, or some sweet, bright picture of flowers, or trees, or trailing, blossoming creepers. It was a place to make happiness itself happier; to turn unrest into perfect calm; to help to soothe any trouble; uplift the gloom from any hour of sorrow; upraise the mind and heart in almost any moment of heaviness, or lowness, or inaptness for pleasures pure and true. To a man like Canon Godfrey it was a veritable 'earthly paradise,' a place to be grateful for at all times, to look upon with an especial gratitude in hours of discouragement or self-depreciation. And many such hours were known to the Canon, as they are to all souls that are pure and true, and live by aspiration.

He was a man of influence—an influence

which had spread beyond his own immediate neighbourhood. Though he was, comparatively speaking, a young man, that is considering the dignity of the position he had arrived at in the Church, people came to him from afar with troubles, difficulties, perplexities, spiritual and temporal, and few went away but went with lighter heart or clearer brain, though now and then one went with heavier conscience than before. Canon Godfrey was a man who had no tenderness for sin, no sympathy with continuance in wrong-doing. Expediency was a word he did not understand.

You had only to see his face once to perceive the bravery written there. The broad, unfurrowed brow had yet a stamp of vigorous resolution; the mouth, half-hidden by a short moustache, and the square chin, were visibly marked by strength and determination. And yet the face was not hard—the reverse of that. The kind, blue eyes alone would have redeemed it from any suspicion of hardness or harshness. And now and then a singular expression would pass over the handsome countenance, an indefinable something that seemed not only to win your admiration for the man, but your love, and even your compassion. Had some great sorrow left its touch there ? or was the passing claim upon your pathos prophetic of sorrow to come ?

As it has been said, it was only now and then that this sadder expression was upon his face. His usual look was one of extreme openness, of gladness and brightness subdued by the never-failing consciousness that his life was being lived in the presence of that life's Giver. In his merriest and most light-hearted moments—and they were not few—*that* look was in the thoughtful blue eyes—the look that told of recollectedness.

The consultation between the Canon and his wife as to whether or no Thorhilda should be allowed to go over to Garlaff Grange on a mission of remonstrance to her brother Hartas, was a prolonged one, and included side questions of some importance.

'What, precisely, does Thorda wish to do?' the Canon asked. He was sitting by the broad window-sill of his study, leaning his head upon his hand in thoughtfulness. 'What is she thinking, or fearing?'

'She is fearing that one of two things will

happen,' replied Mrs. Godfrey, speaking with graver face and voice than usual. 'Either that Hartas will marry Barbara Burdas, or that he will trifle with her—win her affection, and then leave her to her misery. Thorhilda hopes to be able to persuade him to break off the——well, let us say the acquaintanceship, at once.'

'Does she think that Hartas really cares for the girl?'

'She is persuaded that he cares intensely; that is the difficulty. All her hope lies in the idea that Barbara does not yet care greatly for him. She means to try to influence them both.'

Canon Godfrey was silent for a while; but it was an eloquent silence. His wife knew that he was thinking deeply.

'I am not sure that I should consider Hartas's marriage to Barbara Burdas such a great calamity,' he said presently.

'*My dear Hugh!*' exclaimed his wife. Her astonishment precluded further speech.'

'Think of it!' said the Canon gravely. 'You would never wish him to remain unmarried—that would round his chances of ruin as few other things would do. And what kind of wife can you expect him to win? I do not forget that I am speaking of your nephew; and I speak precisely as I should of any relation of my own—you know that, Milicent; and therefore I can ask you to think seriously of his utter want of culture, of his idleness, his rough manner; and last, but not least, of his utter pennilessness. He is Squire Theyn's son, I grant you; but what woman, in what the world would call his own rank of life, would marry him? It may seem a hard saying, but, so far as I can perceive, it would not be at all a bad thing that he should marry a woman of the working class. His very surroundings would then impel him to work himself; he would be happier, stronger, and he would be a better and more respectable member of society. . . . But these are extempore thoughts, my dear Milicent. Therefore don't let them disturb you.'

'You will not mention them to Thorhilda yet awhile?'

'Certainly not. I shall expect her to do all she can to avert the threatened catastrophe. There are many other things to be said.

Society is so constituted nowadays that it would not be at all needful for Hartas to make such a violent descent in the social scale. I could name half-a-dozen good girls in the neighbourhood more suitable than Bab Burdas. There are the three daughters of Stephens, at the saw-mills, then there is Annie Prior, and there are Grace and Agnes Young. No; he need not go to the limpet-rocks for a wife. Still I have, and always have had, a high opinion of Barbara Burdas. There is more in her than meets the eye at the first moment, and beyond all doubt she is attractive, strongly and strikingly attractive. It is in Hartas's favour that he should be drawn to admire a woman of such force of character.'

'Yet you would hardly wish to call her your niece?'

The Canon saw that his wife was moved to a greater extent than she wished to betray. Her face was flushed, her lips slightly tremulous. The moment was a weighty one to both.

'I should not,' the Canon replied; 'but I half-suspect myself in making the admission. I am no Radical, as you know, but a staunch and loyal Conservative, with a firm belief in the fact that social differences—differences of wealth, rank, and position—are part of a divinely-ordered plan. *It is childish to suppose otherwise*—childish and unscriptural. The roots of all such differences are innate, and not to be done away by any merely human legislation. The foolish people who suppose that the nationalisation of the land, the dispersion of capital, the equalization of wealth would change the order of things permanently, must be strangely incapable of looking beyond to-morrow. Put all humanity on one level—so far as the possession of wealth is concerned—this afternoon, and by this day week we should find ourselves more widely separated than ever before. Yet, do not mistake me, do not suppose that I am satisfied with things as they are; do not for one moment imagine that I can look upon, or think upon, the poor of the land, the poor at our very gate, and not be filled with compunction, nay, with remorse. I have thought much of these things of late; I hope to think much more; and I cannot tell whither I may be led and guided. All my prayer is that I may have strength to obey whatever light may be given me. I feel strongly that I am on the verge of some spiritual and human crisis; and it is thought of and knowledge of the condition of the poor of England that have led me to this critical verge. I cannot speak now of my thought, of my aim, of my aspiration; I cannot tell you now how I yearn to be instrumental, were it but ever so slightly, in bringing about a better order of things, a reconcilement of ideas, a union of hopes, an amelioration of the actual present condition of " poor humanity." But you will understand that I cannot look with quite your horror upon the thing you are dreading. I have said that I have no desire to call Barbara Burdas my niece, yet I trust that I should exhibit no unmanly or unChristian pride if I were called upon to acknowledge the relationship. My ideas want readjusting.'

'If yours need readjustment, what must other people's need?'

'I cannot tell—I cannot tell! And I am, in a certain sense, responsible for so many people's ideas. The thought is appalling. It comes to me in the night when I wake, and I grow hot with the sudden pressure of conscience; and then the weight of dread chills me and I sleep. Is it typical—the night's programme? Can it be? I pray that it may not! Come what may, I trust that my soul will never sleep, nor words of mine lull any other soul to sleep. . . . I am always glad to see that Thorda's conscience is quick enough with regard to her own people.'

'Quick enough! I fear it is only too quick,' replied Mrs. Godfrey with enthusiasm. 'If you had seen her face yesterday morning you would not think it needful to harrow her feelings about such a worthless weed as her brother Hartas.'

'Milicent! That is not like you!'

'I know it is not. Forgive me! But when I think of the way in which he has received your most kindly advice and persuasion—to say nothing of my own—and when I remember his lifelong laziness, his insolence, his utter and wilful ignorance, I feel all that is wicked within me stirred to the last dregs. . . . And, oh me! I fear that Rhoda is but very little better.'

'You are not alone in that fear, Milicent. And every now and then there comes across me a sharp pang—have we, after all, striven to the uttermost? One can never know!'

'*You* can never know, Hugh, dear; because you are never satisfied with yourself—do what you may. Think of the manner in which you strove with Rhoda for weeks together after the long illness that she had, three years ago; and when her very life had been despaired of! How you talked to her, and besought her, and prayed with her, and for her, even when she was answering your every word with a sneer. Oh, don't speak of *your* not having done enough. Surely there is a limit to human effort!'

'Ah! but who shall dare to fix it? Not any human being. Think of the long-sufferance one almost expects from God Himself! Think of His exclaiming, by the mouth of His prophet Amos, "*Behold, I am pressed under you as a cart is pressed that is full of sheaves!*" What human experience can be named by the side of that? Oh! don't let us talk of having done enough; rather let us begin again at the beginning, and strengthen one's effort as one perceives greater need for effort. Let Thorda go this afternoon by all means. Her very calmness, her simple, natural elevation, may do more than words can do. Certainly, let her go; let her have such satisfaction as may come from the knowledge that " she has done what she could." '

## CHAPTER VIII.

### AT GARLAFF GRANGE.

'A piteous lot it were to flee from man,
  Yet not rejoice in Nature.'
                                    WORDSWORTH.

THE Grange stood in a deep hollow, surrounded by green folding hills. The sloping fields were each one bordered by hedges of hawthorn, tall straggling hedges with crisp emerald foliage, and scented flowers of creamy white embossing every spray. There were still cattle in the pastures, but they were few and ill-favoured. There were sheep and young lambs, but not of the breed that had once been the pride and boast of Garlaff Grange. In the hill-side paddock at the back of the house, the ancient hack on which the Squire now and then rode to market was grazing at his ease. The garden was shut in by grey stone walls, high and massive, and of quaint style. Below, a road wound round to half-a-dozen labourers' cottages, which stood at the back of the Grange, half-buried among pear and cherry and apple trees. Sweet-briar bushes, mingled with crisp gooseberries, pushed their way through the dilapidated palings, currants shot upward and waved about with the airy lightness of spirit common to unproductive men and things everywhere. The stables were near the cottages, the unsavoury refuse heaps stood in front, and made debatable land for fowls and pigs. Down there in the hollow all was so sunny, so warm, so picturesque, so luxuriant, that a sense of drowsiness seemed the natural and inevitable influence of the place. Thorhilda, stepping from the carriage, seemed certainly as if she stepped into some Lotus Land wherein it was 'always afternoon.'

There was an ancient archway in the wall, filled by a big old oaken door, and then a long pathway under meeting lilacs and laburnums. There were some snowy guelder-roses on either hand, and the rosy mauve of rhododendrons. The broad steps up to the house were moss-grown, the bent and broken railing of wrought iron was half-covered by the young green of climbing rose-trees. A scarlet japonica hung from the wall between the low stone mullioned windows, needing sorely a little kindly pruning and training. This air of neglect was upon everything, upon the panes of the leaded windows upon the steep red-tiled roof, under the eaves where long spires of grass waved in the wooden spouting, stopping the flowing of the rain. The nests of familiar swallows clung to the wall, pigeons cooed upon the roof. All was still, and sad, and sweet, and melancholy.

Though it was the middle of the afternoon the Squire was there by the fireside of the big untidy dining-room. His long clay pipe was in his hand, his tankard of ale before him. His whole air and appearance was that of a man defiant of all opinion, careless of all regard, hopeless of any good, present or future.

That he had once been a man with some claim to be considered fine-looking you saw at a glance, and indeed there was still something in the expression of his face, especially when

the deep grey eyes were lifted to yours
suddenly and seriously, that awoke in you a
kind of wonder, mingled with compassion.
It was an expression that told you that,
whatever the present, the past had not been
wholly bounded by poverty, inner or outer,
by mental lowness, by physical carelessness.
His dress was characteristic. The black
velveteen coat was not new, nor had it
been well-preserved, and yet it had an air
of its own, an air that neither dust nor dirt
could quite destroy; and the corduroy knee-
breeches were not of the kind worn by the
Squire's stable-boy. The finishing touch to
his costume was given by a low, wide-
brimmed, grey felt hat, which he had not
removed when he sat down to his one o'clock
dinner. Though his dead wife's sister, Miss
Averil Chalgrove, and Rhoda, his younger
daughter, had dined at the same table, their
presence had not moved him to any courtesy.
Miss Chalgrove had ceased to expect it long
ago, and Rhoda, never having known her
father to be guilty of weakness of that kind,
would have been surprised to discern any
sign of change. She had no wish for such

change. Things would be very well as they were if only money were not so scarce at the Grange. Very naturally Rhoda craved for more life, more movement, more pleasure, and it may be that the denial of these and other needs had done more to warp a nature not naturally good or lovable than any about her could perceive. No one professed to understand Squire Theyn's youngest daughter.

Rhoda was there in the room and Hartas. Miss Chalgrove had gone 'to lie down,' as her custom was always in the afternoon. How else could she keep that look of youthfulness upon which she prided herself so greatly? It was haste, and impetuosity, and overanxiety that destroyed the looks of nine women out of ten, so she averred, with an emphasis unsuited to the theory she was maintaining. And she added always an expression of her opinion that Garlaff Grange was no fitting home for one so sensitive to roughness, to unrefinement, to unorthodox ways of living as herself. It never had been, but no alternative had been open to her. These facts she dwelt upon in a manner that might have done something toward destroying the harmony of any other household. At the Grange, unhappily, there was no harmony to be destroyed.

They had heard the carriage, this strange trio, and Rhoda had gone to the window as quickly as the movements of her ungainly figure would permit. As she seated herself again she said in a tone of sullen disappointment:

'Nobbut the Princess!'

No one rose when Thorhilda opened for herself the door of the wide, grey, slovenly-looking room. She was smiling pleasantly, trying to look genial, as she glanced from one unsmiling, irresponsive face to another; saying in her lightest and cheeriest tone:

'Good morning, father! good morning, all of you! What a glorious day it is! Surely Aunt Averil could not make up her mind to go and lie down to-day! I thought that perhaps she and you would have gone for a little drive, Rhoda, while I am here.... Would you like to go?'

'Naäy,—Ah care nowt aboot it,' said Rhoda slowly and sullenly, after a somewhat irritating period of hesitation. She was not in the habit of speaking broad Yorkshire except to the Rectory party. By that subtle instinct which such people always seem to possess in perfection, she knew that her use of the dialect in its coarsest form gave annoyance.

But Thorhilda was not to be easily annoyed to-day.

'Then I will have the carriage put up, if I may,' she said, as pleasantly as if no refusal of a kind offer had had to be encountered. 'And perhaps you will give me a cup of tea presently. Hartas, will you please tell Woodward to come round for me at five?—or no, say half-past; that will give me a little longer time.'

Hartas rose slowly, and went out, his pipe still in his mouth, his hands in his pockets; a look of strange indocile determination upon his unformed features.

'Forewarned's forearmed!' he said to himself half-audibly as he went down under the white and purple lilac trees to the front gate to give the message. The two men on the box of the carriage listened, touched their hats respectfully, and turned away, the older man half-sorry for Miss Theyn, whom he had known and liked greatly from her earliest childhood. The younger man was somewhat scornful under his outer respectfulness, and contemptuous of Miss Theyn's brother.

Hartas was less imperceptive, less indifferent than he appeared to be; and his perception did not tend to modify the feeling with which he turned to meet his elder sister, who was coming down the steps, smiling kindly, yet half-sadly, and looking into his face with a beseeching, winning look that would have won any other man's favour in spite of himself.

'Let us go into the orchard, Hartas,' she said, making a movement as if she would put her hand within his arm, but this he evaded skilfully. It was much that he consented to follow her through the narrow door that was all overhung with white blossom and green waving sprays. He was in no mood to bear expostulation.

'Might as well have it over though,' he said to himself. 'An' the sooner the better. But they must'n think, none of 'em, 'at they're goin' to come between me an' Barbara Burdas.'

# CHAPTER IX.

## 'LOVE'S NOBILITY.'

'Man was made of social earth,
　Child and brother from his birth,
　Fettered by the lightest cord
　Of blood thro' veins of kindness poured.
　Next his heart the fireside band
　Of mother, father, children stand ;
　Names from awful childhood heard,
　Throbs of a wild religion stirred.'
　　　　　　　　　　EMERSON.

CURIOUSLY enough, it was Hartas who opened the conversation, rather to Thorhilda's relief. It was not so easy to her to go straight to the heart of this delicate matter as it had appeared to be beforehand; and, in the moment of silence that followed their entrance into the orchard, it seemed to Miss Theyn that she had never before so clearly recognised the strangeness that was between her brother and herself, the absence of all fraternal feeling on his part, the presence of non-sisterly diffidence and trepidation on her own. But, as was usual with her in such crises, she made a strong mental effort to regain her natural standpoint; and the effort was successful. She listened quite calmly to Hartas's opening speech.

'Time's not o' much vally to me,' he began, taking his pipe from his mouth with evident reluctance. 'Therefore I can't say 'at I don't want to waste it. An' as for words, well, I've no special talent i' that direction; as no doubt you've found out afore to-day. Still, I don't want to spend neither words nor time upon the subject you've come here to talk about. It won't do no good, you see, not the least. If Barbara Burdas would but listen to me, an' the law o' the land allowed, I'd marry her to-night. I'd not wait for to-morrow.'

Real earnestness is always impressive, and is as the 'heat which sets our human atoms spinning' in the direction the one in earnest would have us travel. The fervour of a true affection is seldom to be altogether ignored, even by the coldest.

'How long have you cared for her so much?'

Miss Theyn asked in a gentle and sympathetic way. And her very voice, the affectionate unexpected kindness of it, touched Hartas as no remonstrance could have done. All unaware he was already betrayed.

'How long? All my life, or so it seems to me now,' he replied, 'or mebbe I'd better say, all *her* life. Why, it only seems like yesterday 'at she was a little hard-working thing of twelve or fourteen; bright, an' bonny, an' full o' mischief, yet as disdainful as the highest lady o' the land. An' then somehow, all at once it seemed, she came to be eighteen; and——'

'Eighteen!' interposed Thorhilda in amazement. 'I should have said she was at least eight-and-twenty!'

'She looks more like that,' Hartas admitted somewhat sadly. 'But think of the life she's lived for the last six years! Mebbe you don't know nought about it; an' couldn't understand if you did; but *I* know. I've watched her all along when she little thought of it; an' many a time the sight's been bad anuff to bear, I can tell you.'

'What made you think of her first?' Thorhilda asked, still speaking in a tone that told of more than mere kindly interest.

'First of all! That I can hardly say,' Hartas replied with softened voice, and a decided increase of confidingness in his manner. 'I remember when she was a little thing. (I'm ten years older than she is—ten all but three months.) An' I always noticed her when I was down at the Bight. She was so different from the rest somehow, so superior, an' yet so winnin'; an' they all seemed to know it; an' to give in when she was by. . . . An' then that awful storm came; an' I was down on the cliff-top that mornin'. Oh! I'll never forget it!'

'Was that the day her father was drowned?'

'Her father and her mother. . . . But you can't have forgot! Why the whole land rang wi' the stories o' that gale for weeks after!'

'There have been so many gales,' replied Thorhilda deprecatingly. 'And I was younger then; and perhaps less sympathising. But I do remember something of the loss of the *North Star*. . . . Wasn't that the name of the boat that suffered here?'

'It was the name o' one of the boats 'at

was wrecked in Ulvstan Bight that mornin', but it was not the name o' the one 'at belonged mostly to Ephraim Burdas. She was called the *Seamew*. An' a fine boat she was, for her size. I remember her well. Old Ephraim had only pointed her out to me about a week before, telling me how she was the fulfilment of all his hopes, the result of all his long life's toil. She'd cost him over four hundred pounds altogether; an' she was every plank his own save one-eighth part, the single share that Jim Tyas had bought. An' 'twas old Ephraim 'at sailed her; the others never seemed right when the old man wasn't at the helm. An' he'd taken his usual place that night; never dreamin' o' nought happenin' out o' the common. All 'at ever he remembered after was 'at his son, Bab's father, had seemed out o' spirits; an' had never spoken to nobody after they went out o' the Bight till the storm burst upon 'em all of a sudden. 'Twas him 'at first saw it comin', in fact. But you should hear old Ephraim tell the tale.'

'I would rather hear it from you; only make it brief; and not too sad. . . . How many were there in the boat altogether?'

'Only four. As I said, the old man were in the stern; an' they'd shot the lines some nine or ten miles off the land. Then they'd sat down to rest for awhile; an' to pass the darkest time o' the night. 'Twas a fair sort o' mornin'; fine, an' light, an' calm; but about four o'clock, as old Ephraim were leanin' again the side o' the boat, his head upon his hand, half-asleep, all of a sudden he heard his son shoutin':

'"*By heav'n there's a storm upon us! Yonder's a ship flyin' afore the gale, wi' her sails all torn to rags an' ribbons!*"

'The old man couldn't believe it; but he jumped up, an' looked out seaward; an' sure anuff, 'twas as young Ephraim had said. There wasn't a second to be lost. They tried to head the boat for the nearest land—it happened to be Yarva Wyke; but long afore they could reach it the gale broke up the sea; an' Jim Tyas wasn't at all for landin' there. Jim was a chap 'at was allus desperate feared in a storm, so old Ephraim told me; an' he said he'd never seen the man so feared as he was that mornin' when the hurricane was fairly upon 'em. They down with the sail afore they touched the sea-break; but there seemed no chance for 'em; an' afore they'd been tossing upon the edge o' the breakers many minutes a great wave struck the boat, an' knocked the side completely out of her. It appeared to be all over then. Jim cried out, "*Lord, ha' mercy upon my wicked soul this day!*" an' as old Ephraim said, it almost seemed as if Providence had heard him, for the strangest thing happened 'at ever the old man had seen in all his long life. The sea broke away right in front of them in the curiousest manner, an' stood up like walls on either hand; an' they were driven through between as fast as they could go. But the boat was breakin' to bits under 'em every minute; an' at last they were all four tossin' i' that awful sea.

'They could all of 'em swim, better or worse, an' they all reached the rocks, but 'twere in a bad place. The cliff's like a house-end just there; an' though a dozen or more people had gathered on the top of it, they'd neither rope nor ladder; an' the worst of it was young Ephraim's wife was there, Bab's mother, an' she'd three little children clingin' to her gown; an' a four-weeks old baby at her breast; an' she weren't well—hadn't never been since the child was born. An' when she saw the boat's crew just below, clingin' to one another on the narrow ledge under the cliff, the straight wall of rock behind em', an' the rising tide beating upon 'em more furiously every moment, 'twere more than she could bear. Breakin' away fra the little ones all of a sudden, she sprang from the top o' the rock wi' her new-born baby in her arms; an' almost as she struck the water her husband dashed in again after her; an' folks has told me since 'at it was all they could do to keep Bab from makin' a fourth. Nobody could help the three 'at was strugglin' there. They went down, within half-a-dozen yards o' dry land. An' the curiousest part of it all was that little Ailsie washed up, not only alive, but seeming none so much the worse. I helped to catch hold of her, and to give her to Bab. An' that's why Bab cares for her so much, an' can hardly bear to let the little thing out of her sight. . . . Bab was only twelve years old when it all happened; but if she'd been twice twelve she couldn't have been a better mother to the three small lads an' the little girl. But it's no use talkin'. Such as you can never see the good in such a woman as Barbara Burdas. She can't play the piano. I doubt much whether she's ever either heard one, or seen one. An' pickin' flithers for the fishermen of Ulvstan Bight isn't quite such a refined way o' spendin' time as makin' wax-flowers, or crochy antimacassars. No; Bab isn't refined wi' what you an' most others such as you would call refinement— not what you'd call a " lady." But no lady 'at I've ever seen, or ever can see, would lift me out o' the mire as Barbara Burdas could do, if she cared to think about me at all; an' there isn't another woman in the world, 'at I know of, 'at understands what unselfishness means as *she* understands it; not another nowhere 'at lives a life so totally self-sacrificin'. An' the best of it is she doesn't never dream 'at she's doin' aught but what she's bound to do. You couldn't open her eyes, if you tried, to the meanin' o' self an' self-interest. . . . But I said I didn't want to waste no time on this subject, an' here I am, wastin' a whole quarter of an hour.'

'Don't regret it,' Thorhilda replied, using the brevity that comes of over-fulness of new thought. Hartas's vividly told story, the graphic touches of it, the intense reality, had impressed his sister greatly. And that in communicating to her his knowledge of Barbara Burdas and her life he should at the same time have betrayed much that was new, and not unfavourable, of himself, was a fact demanding consideration.

'I am glad to hear all this from *you*, Hartas,' she continued. 'I am pleased that you should talk to me about Barbara Burdas.'

'An' you'll be glad if I'll lissen to what you've got to say in return,' the young man broke in with some impetuosity. 'But remember what I said at the beginning. I mean to make her my wife if she will but consent—consent on any terms.'

'And if she will not?'

'If she won't, I don't care what becomes of me.'

'I don't want to preach to you, Hartas,' Thorhilda replied with some natural diffidence, 'but is that altogether a manly mood in which to meet one of the greatest crises that can happen in your lifetime?'

'Manly? Mebbe not. But I reckon 'at you don't know much o' what such a disappointment 'ud mean to me—if it came to that. An' you an' all your set 'ud be rejoicin', as if something good had happened.'

'Can you put yourself in our place for a moment—in *my* place, for instance?' Thorhilda asked with gentle firmness. 'Can you even try to imagine what such a marriage would be to me, what it would mean to my life, were you, my only brother, to marry a— a bait-gatherer?'

'It needn't mean no more to you than the wind that blows!' Hartas replied, with his rough, ready emphasis. 'Why should you think it would? Why should we ever come near you? When have I ever come in your way, except when I couldn't help it? When have I ever asked a favour of you? When have I ever expected so much as a kind word from you, or a helpful one, when I was particularly needing it? What have I ever asked, or requested of you at all, save 'at you should go your way an' leave me to go mine?'

'You have requested nothing—that is true enough,' Thorhilda replied, involuntarily subduing her voice to the softest and gentlest contrast possible. 'But, remember, the difference between us was never created by me, nor by anyone at the Rectory. You must admit that my aunt and uncle have done what they could. And you must also admit that, though you have repulsed them time after time, they have never ceased to make fresh advances. Be generous, at least in word; as they have been in deed. . . . But, pardon me, I am saying more than I meant to say. I do not want to irritate you—anything but that. But I felt constrained to say that all the coldness and strangeness has been your doing, not mine—not ours. It has pained me ceaselessly and infinitely. It has hurt me, and kept me from my sleep; it has darkened many a day; poisoned many a pleasure. . . . Hartas—do you think that I have *no* affection for you?'

It was a singular scene. That a woman of Miss Theyn's stateliness and loveliness, of her extreme refinement, should stand there pleading for some sign of recognition of the tie that was between herself and the man who seemed as the veriest clod by her side, was surely a touching and pathetic thing. Was Hartas feeling it to be strange? Was he moved in any way?—impelled to any warmth of responsiveness that he yet had no art or intellect to express?

'It's a bad moment to speak o' such a thing now,' he said, having less of his natural harshness and brusqueness of manner than before. 'I don't doubt but that you may feel more like a sister to me than I ever dreamed you did; an' at another time I might ha' been glad of it. But, as I said, I know what's brought you here this afternoon; an' I've only one answer to all you have said, or can say. That answer you've had. I won't anger you wi' sayin' it again.'

Thorhilda was silent for awhile. One thing she had to congratulate herself upon—nay, two moved her to a momentary content. She had not irritated her brother; and she had a hopeful feeling of having opened a way that might some day lead to his heart.

'I hope your time has not been quite

wasted, Hartas,' she replied. 'I should certainly not consider that it has been if we might begin to realize, but ever so faintly, that we each owe something to the other—some help, some sympathy, some affection, or, at least, some friendliness of feeling. . . . Has it ever occurred to you that *I* could feel lonely?—that *I* have no brother or sister, except in name?'

Hartas Theyn's face was lifted in most earnest surprise.

'*You* lonely!' he exclaimed. 'No; when I've thought about you at all I've thought that if ever anybody in this world did have all they wanted it was you.'

'Then, ah, how you have been mistaken!' Thorhilda replied with some emphasis. 'Don't imagine that I complain. I am much too conscious of the good that is mine to do that; but my life has not been perfect in its happiness—how should it? You little dream of what I have felt in other people's houses—homes where there may have been a dozen, or half-a-dozen brothers and sisters, all kind, all loving, all happy! Ah! how often it has pained me to see it all—to see it from outside, as a wanderer may sit on a doorstep on a winter's night and see the warmth and light within, which he may not feel or share! I am not blaming you—I am blaming no one. I am merely telling you how it has been with me—how it is yet. I want you to understand how it is, even now.'

'I don't see that I can help matters much,' Hartas replied, not sullenly or indifferently, but with the perplexed absence of one absorbed in thought.

'I have thought that you might—some day,' Thorhilda said. 'I have so often thought of your marriage, so often dreamed of your wife as one who would be my sister, who would draw us together, who would make me feel that I was your sister in reality. And I have seen her in my mind many a time, a good, loving, understanding woman, with— pardon me for saying it—culture enough to be a friend to me, and love enough to bear with all shortcomings in you. . . . And now, now my dream is ended. . . . What wonder that I should plead with you, entreat you, at least, to consider, to do nothing in haste!'

Perhaps it was fortunate that at that

moment Rhoda came up under the white orchard trees. Her appearance might have been amusing to anyone in a mood to be amused lightly; but to Thorhilda all was distressing, from the heavy rolling gait to the untidy tweed dress, unfastened at the throat, yet displaying no finishing touch in the shape of lace or linen collar. Her pretty golden hair was huddled into a shapeless coil at the back of her head; there was a sullen expression about the large mouth, and in the greenish hazel eyes. Her voice was in keeping, being gruff, indistinct, unpleasant.

'If ya want that tea, it's ready,' she said, stopping short of her elder sister and brother by some yards.

Then she turned and rolled back again. Thorhilda sighed and followed her. The visit was over, and it had availed nothing.

'Nothing at all!' she said to herself sadly.

'Nothing, nothing at all!' she repeated to the Canon, who was walking thoughtfully up and down under the veranda at the Rectory when she returned, waiting to console her, or to rejoice with her, as occasion might require.

And now, as always, his consolation was sufficiently effective.

'Be patient, Thorda, dear, and don't despair,' he said, holding her hand in his warm, fatherly grasp. 'The most far-seeing of us can't see the length of the next hour, or the full meaning of this. . . . And now go and dress quickly and prettily; there are some of your favourite pale yellow pansies to wear. The Merediths will be here in twenty minutes.'

# CHAPTER X.

'IN ALL TIME OF OUR WEALTH.'

'Dear friend—If I were sure of thee, sure of thy capacity, sure to match my mood with thine, I should never again think of trifles in relation to thy comings and goings. . . . . Thou art to me a delicious torment. Thine ever, or never.'
EMERSON.

THE dinner-party at the Rectory was quite a small one. Mrs. Meredith, handsome, correct, more affable than usual, sat at Canon Godfrey's right hand. Her son Percival was next to Miss Theyn. Gertrude Douglas, Thorhilda's friend, had been taken in to dinner by the Rev. Marcus Egerton, the one curate of Market Yarburgh.

Gossip had been busy about the four last-mentioned names for some time; but, as usual, the suggestions and hints that had been passed about were at least premature. Miss Theyn, as we have seen, was by no means sure even of her own wish and will, and Miss Douglas was not a likely woman to marry a poor curate. She was older than Thorhilda, taller, stronger, and perhaps equally beautiful in the eyes of some, though in quite a different way, and she was certainly more ambitious. Being the daughter of a not too successful country surgeon, she had a very natural dread of small means.

'I must marry,' she had said openly to Thorhilda, 'and I must marry a rich man. I have had enough of poverty!'

'But you would not marry anyone merely because he was rich?' Thorhilda had asked in unfeigned surprise.

'I fear I should,' Gertrude made answer, speaking half-sadly and tentatively. She had no wish to shock Miss Theyn, though often she came nearer to doing so than she dreamed. 'I fear I should,' she had replied. 'Market Yarburgh is not a place to afford one many chances. I am nearly thirty, and I look older than I am. . . . But don't let us talk of it at present, dear. Let us speak of *your* chances rather than of mine. There is not another Percival Meredith in the neighbourhood.'

Miss Douglas had perceived without being able quite to comprehend Miss Theyn's flush of mingled annoyance and indignation. Not even a friend so intimate as Gertrude Douglas might speak of a matter so delicate, so immature, without offending her sense of good taste.

'My chances!' she exclaimed. 'If you care for me, Gertrude, if you care for my friendship in the least, you will hardly speak so again to me. Indeed, indeed, I thought you had known me better than to speak like that!'

This had happened some time before. Gertrude had laughed most musically, most good-naturedly, and had kissed away Thorhilda's offended dignity at once. There was a peculiar fascination about Miss Douglas; she never took offence, and she was cleverer than Thorhilda in many ways; she had wider knowledge of the world, keener insight into certain sides of human nature; her manner was full of charm, and her temperament most cheerful and amiable. If these good qualities had some alloy, Thorhilda was not one to dwell upon the fact. Gertrude Douglas was her friend, and perfect loyalty requires that even thought itself should be silent now and then.

Gertrude came often to the Rectory. She appreciated the pleasant little dinner-parties; not only the varied *menu*, the delicate cookery, the careful service, but also the beautiful silver, the lovely flowers that decorated the table and the rooms in such profusion, the perfect lighting, the general air of daintiness and finish that was upon everything. Her own narrow home was sadly apt to seem narrower after a few days in the wider rooms in the house on the hill-top; the very carpets seemed dingier and poorer, the chairs harder, the sofas more uncomfortable; the meals were hardly worth sitting down to. As a matter of course she kept silence as to her appreciation; she had too much tact to speak of such matters, except now and then to Thorhilda alone. For social life she had enough of other and brighter topics, and to-night, as usual, she gave sufficient rein to her conversational powers without seeming to display them in any undue manner. No awkward pauses might happen at any table to which Miss Douglas had been invited.

After dinner, while the two elder ladies sat chatting by the fire in the drawing-room, Thorhilda and Gertrude stood near the window in the dim twilight, the hour that so often attunes two waiting souls to helpful intercourse; we owe more, spiritually, than we acknowledge, to the physical alternation of night and day.

The curtains by that especial west window had been left undrawn, as usual, by Thorhilda's wish. Outside the stars were burning in a clear, dark sky; a young moon was dropping over the towers of the ruin on the opposite hill-top; beyond the moon there was a faint, white mist overspreading the distance; the whole scene was touched by that mystery of mingled light and darkness which makes so much of the poetry of this most poetic world. And yet the poetry is often tinged with sadness; the sadness of all *suggested* beauty. It is in music of almost every kind; it is not absent from any good picture; but it is in the natural world that one feels its charm most strongly and strangely. The first morning hour when the light as it were breathes upon the east, the last evening hour, when it seems to sigh itself gently and sadly away, the calm, stirless moonlight, the soft, wondrous glowing of the winter starlight over the wide expanse of moor or of sea; all these in their tender disclosures, their mystic reservations, move the soul to 'strange yearnings after we know not what, and awful impressions from we know not whence.' The wise man is he who seeks these finer influences frequently, and having found them, acknowledges with gratitude that it is 'good to be there.'

The two younger women were still standing silently, but Miss Douglas broke the silence so soon as she felt it.

'Thorda, dear, you are not happy to-night!' she said in her round, full, musical voice, a voice difficult to soften at any time.

Thorhilda smiled, and lifted her face to her friend.

'It is odd that you should make that remark,' she replied, in tones that contrasted perfectly with those of Gertrude Douglas. 'All day, nay, for quite two days now, I have found myself thinking of happiness at every spare moment, and this by no deliberate wish or will of my own. Is it not strange?'

'Very. . . . But surely you are happy enough? What happiness you haven't yet is coming toward you as fast as it can come. No, don't turn your face away, dear, I won't say another word. I couldn't help sitting opposite to you at dinner, you know; neither could I help seeing Mr. Meredith's face, or hearing his voice. There—I've done!'

'Of that I'm glad. . . . But, Gertrude, you mistake me altogether. It was not only of my own happiness I was thinking, but of that of other people—of the whole human race in fact. We all want to be happy; we are, many of us, striving for it; yet surely we none of us know very exactly what happiness is!'

While Gertrude was laughing, a long, low, pleasant laugh, the Canon and the two younger men came in, and involuntarily began to smile for very sympathy with the musical sound that was coming from the window.

'Just at the right moment!' cried Miss Douglas. 'Do come here, all of you, and tell us what happiness is! Here is Thorhilda miserable because she can't make out what happiness consists of. Isn't it an idea?'

Miss Douglas had sauntered out from the

recess by the window as she spoke, coming forth with that half-imperious air of conscious fascination that became her so well. And in the background of her thought, of which she was also conscious, was a curious query as to whether in the sight of—say Percival Meredith, for instance—she or Thorhilda made the most attractive picture.

They were nearly alike in height, in a certain cultured air of self-possession, but there, suddenly, all possibility of comparison ended. Their very dress told something of the radical difference of their natures. Miss Douglas's costume of amber satin and black lace, with a profusion of yellow roses, grown under the Rectory glass, was sufficiently æsthetic even for the taste of Mr. Meredith, but it did not charm him as did the soft heliotrope-tinted crape that Thorhilda was wearing, with only a few pale primrose-coloured pansies and some maidenhair by way of ornament.

He felt a little proud of his superior taste. But in justice to him let it be said that it was not only the outer appearance of the woman he loved that attracted him; this by no means. He was sufficiently cultured to feel the drawing of the finer nature, the more finished delicacy. As to whether or not he might find himself in perfect agreement with a deeper soul or more aspiring spirit, was not a question likely to trouble him as yet. So far no doubt of this kind had beset him.

# CHAPTER XI.

### CONCERNING HAPPINESS.

> 'He could afford to suffer
> With those whom he saw suffer. Hence it came
> That in our best experience he was rich,
> And in the wisdom of our daily life.'
> 
> WORDSWORTH.

'HAPPINESS!' Percival Meredith ejaculated softly, as he drew away toward the window, turning with a self-possessed air, as of invitation, to Thorhilda. Then lower still and more emphatically he said, 'I know what would make *my* happiness!'

But for Miss Douglas it is possible that Thorhilda's eyes had yet been so far closed as to permit of her replying to this remark as it was intended to be replied to, with some 'soft nothing' that would provide an opening for a stronger and less dubious declaration. As it was, the nothing could not be uttered at that moment. Instead, Miss Theyn said aloud :

'Uncle Hugh, what is your idea of happiness? You are the happiest man I know.'

A touch of gravity came over the Canon's face, into the blue, kindly eyes; the smile faded from about the mouth.

'I *am* happy,' he said, 'and I am glad to acknowledge it; but it is not an unshaded happiness. How should it be, when I fear that—taking the world about us generally—not one person in a hundred could say the same thing! . . . As to *defining* happiness—who could give any true and generally acceptable definition of the word? It is probable that to each human being it means some totally different thing. Not one of us could legislate for another so far as merely human happiness is concerned.'

'I should say the best definition is "having all one wants,"' Gertrude Douglas replied with her usual readiness.

'That *seems* adequate,' said the Canon. 'And yet if by that you mean the gratification of all material desires, I can only reply that I know men who have not a single desire unfulfilled, but who are yet far enough from happiness. On the other hand, I know people, ground down under what men term the heel of Fate, poor, lonely, bereaved, neglected, but yet as bright, as cheerful, as hopeful as any human being need wish to be.'

'Ah, if they have *hope?*' said Mr. Egerton, in his usual suggestive way.

'You think that is the great secret?' the Canon asked. 'And *you*, Mr. Meredith—where does your opinion lie?'

Percival smiled languidly.

'Upon my word, I don't know that I've ever thought of it, either one way or another,' he said. 'Just now, when Miss Douglas was speaking, I felt decidedly inclined to agree with her. But I should fancy there's a good deal to be said for Egerton's idea. Why not combine the two—have everything you want, and something to hope for besides? Then, surely, you would touch something like real felicity!'

Canon Godfrey looked at his neighbour with something that was almost curiosity, and for a few seconds he made no reply. His best and most spiritual thoughts on this topic seemed hardly suited to the present environment.

'It is probable,' he said at last, 'that a true answer to the question asked in the beginning would draw upon the deepest resources of the nature of each one of us, and it would be no bad theme for an hour's quiet meditation to try to find an answer. The queries need only be three : I. Am I happy ? II. If not, then *why?* III. What can I do to bring happiness somewhat nearer ?'

'Let us do it now! and each of us write down our answer!' exclaimed Miss Douglas in her sparkling, ready way.

But Thorhilda protested instantly.

'Oh no, *no!*' she cried. 'I could not do that, not now. I could not make a game of it, *pour passer le temps!* . . . Forgive me, Gertrude; but I could not, I could not tonight.'

'Oh, dear; how terribly in earnest we are!' exclaimed Miss Douglas smiling—nay, laughing quite sweetly. 'One never expects to have to take things *au sérieux* after dinner!'

'I fear we are some of us talking great

nonsense!' interposed practical little Mrs. Meredith. She was being ignored in a way she was not accustomed to. The very set of her imposing cap upon her most abundant and artistic white hair told you that she was not a person to be overlooked. She was as full of life, of vigour, as she had always been, and the snow-white hair was as surprising as it was picturesque. In spite of it, she did not look more than forty, though her age was fifty-five; and that her only son should already be giving himself some of the airs of a middle-aged man was not pleasing to her. The surest way for a stranger to reach her heart was to make some allusion to 'her brother.' 'I fear we are talking nonsense,' she repeated. 'For my part, I think happiness is very much a matter of mental habit. George Eliot admits something like that. Does she not say somewhere that " unhappiness may become a habit of mind "? And doubtless such habits are very hard to break.'

'There is truth in that,' replied the Canon. 'But surely, before sorrow can become so habitual as to be more congenial than joy, any human being must have bent to discipline both long and sore, and, in such cases, which of us, not having sounded the same depths, shall dare to judge?'

'Oh, but we always *do* judge one another,' the little woman broke in with something that seemed more like hardness than flippancy in her tone. 'We can't help it; and when we see people whose troubles are over, but who yet *won't* forget them, you know we can't help thinking they want a little more trouble to bring them to their senses . . . . Oh, don't pretend, Canon Godfrey, you know you agree with me!'

'I certainly won't pretend,' replied the Canon, smiling gravely, and putting away into the background of his mind some stern experiences of which he knew only too much. 'No, I won't pretend; instead, I will add to what you have urged. I have a firm belief that a sense of happiness is a thing to be cultivated, a sense of daily and hourly gratitude for our human well-being, let the drawbacks be what they may. I fear that there are people in whom this sense is so imperfectly developed that it can hardly be said to exist at all! . . . Don't you think that is true, Egerton?'

'Only too true!' responded Mr. Egerton with his usual quick appreciation, giving you an impression of a human mind all alight because of the warmth of heart not hidden within. 'Indeed, I have often fancied that we might have a new Professor—a Professor of the Art of Happiness—a man with psychological knowledge enough to do for our emotional half what the physiologist is endeavouring to do for our bodies; a man who would go on his daily rounds to this house, or to that, as a doctor does; finding out this woman's reason for habitual sadness, the cause of that man's gloomy despair; who would analyse our feelings for us, put them into definite shape, and then put before us the unphilosophical view we were taking so strongly and clearly as to change the whole mental atmosphere. It might be done, surely!'

It was easy to see that Mr. Egerton had only meant to be taken half-seriously. But the Canon, listening, had passed on into earnest.

'Are we not trying to do it—some of us?' he asked. 'Trying to do just that—to minister to minds diseased wherever we may find them? It is not easy; how should it be? We have high authority for believing that each heart alone knows its own bitterness, that no other heart can know it, or share it. Think of Keble, too:

> '"Not even the tenderest heart, and next our own,
>   Knows half the reasons why we smile or sigh."

Of course it doesn't; how should it? And the most closely-surrounded heart is lonelier than we know. How, then, must it be with those who, admittedly, have not a single soul to whom they can unburden themselves for an hour? It is cases like these one is glad to find out, to help, not heeding the difficulties. If one may not create happiness, one may, at least now and then, alleviate unhappiness. And that is not a little; no, it is certainly not a little in the sight of Him who said, "*Inasmuch as ye did it unto one of the least of these, ye did it unto Me.*"'

'Won't you give us a sermon on happiness some Sunday, Uncle Hugh?' Thorhilda asked gravely.

'Certainly I will, or else a lecture in the schoolroom some Wednesday evening. The latter will be better; even on your own showing, my dear! It is not so long since you admitted that sermons were difficult things to listen to.'

'So they are *to me!*' Miss Theyn admitted, preparatory to asking yet another leading question on the topic just begun. But before the question could be put into suitable and sufficiently earnest words, Gertrude Douglas had changed the subject altogether. It was a way she had. For all her tact she knew little of the decaying art of conversation.

And for Percival Meredith, too, the evening was spoiled, that is, so far as his one intention was concerned. It yet remained to him to ask formally for an interview on the morrow, and though he thought seriously on this, he put the idea away rather impatiently at last. It seemed to belong to a past day; and Percival was anxious, beyond even his natural years, to keep pace with the present. The fact that he was so much older than Miss Theyn had more than its due weight with him. The difference would have been as nothing to a man who had not, in some way, passed the ' slow feet' of the years.

And yet his mood that night was by no means a sad one. He sat alone in his smoking room for some time, half-wishing that he had asked Mr. Egerton to come over to Ormston for a few days, and half-glad that he had not.

'Still,' he said to himself, 'when one is in a state of perplexity, or suspense, solitude is seldom quite welcome.' Then he chose for himself a good cigar, and poked the fire into a blaze, and put up the Berlin slippers which his mother had worked with such extreme care to be thoroughly toasted. 'And yet, why *should* I be perplexed?' he said to himself when these arrangements for his personal comfort had been made to his satisfaction. 'I know what I wish to do, and what I mean to do; then why perplexity? . . . And as for suspense?' . . . and here Mr. Meredith took his cigar from between his lips and smiled satirically. 'Suspense! with a lady so dainty and so shy, waiting in her utmost daintiness and shyness for one to throw the handkerchief. Well, it is certainly not—not altogether unpleasant! One might — at Market Yarburgh—bide one's time, and make a successful throw after all! That is one advantage of a country place. . . . And there are others — several others ! . . . At the present moment I am in love with Ormston Magna.'

# CHAPTER XII.

### IN THE VILLAGE STREET.

'Can another be so blessed, and we so pure, that we can offer him tenderness? When a man becomes dear to me I have touched the goal of fortune.'—EMERSON.

THEY were roses, lovely fresh roses that filled Miss Theyn's hands. She was alone in the carriage as it drove down one of the narrow streets of Ulvstan—streets where greengrocers lived, and pastry-cooks, and vendors of bathing garments. Thorhilda had no purchases to make, and the roses were intended for the matron of the small cottage hospital which the Canon had done so much towards instituting, and now maintained almost solely by his own generosity. But the roses never reached Mrs. Nesbitt. A tall figure, bearing a basket covered with seaweed, suddenly turned the corner of the street — a blue worsted-clad figure, with no bonnet to hide the coils of her beautiful chestnut hair, no hat to shade the finely-cut features upon which the cast of thought was already marked so plainly. Miss Theyn saw the girl, recognised her, and stopped the carriage instantly. A moment's reflection might perhaps have changed her feeling, but that moment was not possible. Thorhilda was acting and speaking out of her first impulse.

'Barbara,' she cried, holding out the big bouquet of lovely roses, red, creamy-white, deep crimson, and palest blush. 'Barbara! will you have these? They are quite fresh. And how is your grandfather? My uncle fancied he was not looking quite so well as usual at church on Sunday morning.'

The tide of rich colour that was pouring over Bab's face, under her hair, down her neck, attested the confusion to which she was moved by the suddenness of the encounter; but no muscle of her beautiful, regular features was tortured to express her emotion. The girl lifted her gray-blue eyes—there was no sauciness in them now, no defiance; there was nothing but a deep and deferential admiration—nay, it was more, affection, devotion, as Miss Theyn saw. And the girl stood like a statue for calmness and for dignity, taking the bouquet—such a one as she had never seen before—and, apart from the fact that Miss Theyn had given it to her, the roses were in themselves as precious as any pearls or diamonds Bab's limited experience enabled her to imagine. The blushes continued to grow upon the fine face, but Bab was not speechless.

'You mean them for me?' she said, using a soft, grave surprise that was as touching as it was welcome. Her eyes were drooping over the flowers, her lips a little tremulous with the weight of pleasure.

'How will I thank you, Miss Theyn?' she added. 'How will I ever thank you? An' there's nothing I can do, nothing!'

'You hardly need to thank me, not for a few flowers,' Miss Theyn replied; and it was easy to see that she was receiving almost as much pleasure as she was giving. 'Do you care for them so much? I am glad of that. I can bring you some often, almost every time we come into Ulvstan.'

'Oh, don't think of that, Miss Theyn,' Bab replied, her independence taking quick alarm at the idea of a pleasure so spontaneous being converted into a benefit 'to be continued.' 'Don't think of that,' she said; 'I'll never forget as you've given me these.'

Thorhilda was quick to understand.

'Very well!' she said, with one of her usual winning smiles. 'I think I know what you feel, and I will respect it. All the same, I may come and see you, I hope? I have been promising myself that pleasure.'

The blush on Barbara's face deepened; and since the words she could have said—words of gratitude for even the hope of some crumbs of affection—since these might not be spoken, she had few others, and these were not adequate.

'I'd like to see you,' she said, lifting her truthful eyes to Miss Theyn's face; 'I'd like to see you often—every day of my life if it might be. But——'

Bab hesitated here, and looked somewhat embarrassed; and while she was silent a probable cause for her sudden hesitation crossed Miss Theyn's mind.

'You are not afraid that I might try to influence you against your wish, are you, Barbara?' she asked. 'Are you thinking, for instance, that I may try to persuade you to discountenance my brother? Is it that?'

Barbara lifted her straightforward, unsuspicious face, and some pain was written there, some surprise.

'No,' she said, 'I was not thinking o' that, not then. But since you have spoke of it of yoursel', Miss Theyn, would you mind sayin' more—all you think, indeed?'

'All that I think on the matter,' Thorhilda said earnestly; 'that would be difficult. Still I should like you to know the truth. . . . Let us speak exactly. I went over to the Grange one day on purpose to speak to my brother about you; it was the day after I had seen you on the beach. I went to talk to him about his intercourse with you, to ask him his wishes and intentions, to beg him to consider seriously what he was doing. But afterward when I came away, and was trying to remember what I had said, I was surprised to find that I had said so little of all that I had meant to say. . . . Life is seldom cut and squared to one's anticipations. Some new experience, giving rise to some new feeling, does away with all the old conclusions, and one is left perplexed.'

Bab was listening, fully understanding, and Miss Theyn knew that she understood. Half unaware, an opinion as to Bab's quick and strong intellectual capacity was growing within her with every turn of the conversation. It was not what the girl said, but what the expression of her face said for her.

'Let us speak exactly, you said just now, Miss Theyn;' and Bab's repetition of the phrase, her very intonation of it, might have been amusing at another time. 'Let us speak exactly, you say. Well, then, you did wish to persuade your brother from thinkin' o' me. You went to the Grange on purpose?'

'Yes,' Miss Theyn replied, sorry for the sudden sorrow she saw in Barbara's eyes and about the finely-curved, sensitive mouth. Barbara remained quite silent.

'I did go on that errand,' Miss Theyn repeated. 'But I must tell you all; I must tell you that I found my brother's mind so completely made up that no influence of mine availed to move him from his purpose for a second. . . . We are a stubborn race, we of Garlaff, and we seldom change.'

'Then you failed of your erran'!' Bab asked quietly.

'Yes; utterly.'

'An' you were sorry?'

'How shall I reply to that, Barbara? I wish to tell the truth, and I do not wish to pain you.'

'And the truth is——'

'The truth is simply this,' interrupted Miss Theyn, not liking to see any longer the sad, heart-hungry look on Bab's face—it was like watching the going down of some emotional thermometer, marking the degrees of lowering disappointment. 'The truth is this, that I do not at present understand myself, my own feeling in the matter. . . . I suppose I had some regret; I suppose I did feel some annoyance at my brother's strong determination.'

'Thank you, Miss Theyn,' Barbara said very calmly. 'I knew you'd speak plain, an' I'm glad you spoke to-day. . . . An' thank you again for the roses. 'Twas good of you, an' kind, to give them to me.'

Barbara's face had grown paler as she turned away; her look was grave to dignity, and her bow graceful enough for any lady in the land. Thorhilda bowed and smiled, then gave a word to the coachman, who was glad that his impatient horses should at last be delivered from that long stay in the village street. 'Home,' Miss Theyn said, throwing herself back among the rugs and cushions, and yielding herself up to feelings of mingled dissatisfaction and self-reproach. In wishing to be perfectly truthful, had she gone beyond the truth? Had she been quite careful enough of the evidently too-sensitive feelings of another? Barbara Burdas had touched her, appealed to the yet but half-awakened sense of humanity that was struggling for its existence within her, and she could not put away the appeal.

'I wish I had said a word more—but one word!' she exclaimed half-audibly. 'Perhaps I may say it yet—I must. That sad look of Barbara's will certainly haunt me so long as it is unsaid!'

# CHAPTER XIII.

### EXTENUATING CIRCUMSTANCES.

'Well you may, you must, set down to me,
Love that was life,—life that was love.'
ROBERT BROWNING.

WAS it a little unfortunate that Hartas should take it into his head to go down to Ulvstan that same evening? He had not seen Barbara for some days; he was feeling lonely and unhappy, and also unhopeful; and the unexpected darkness and chilliness of the summer night helped his feeling of depression. And he soon discerned that Bab was not likely to put it away that evening. He recognised at once that she was in some highly-wrought mood not to be accounted for by failure or success in gathering her tale of limpets.

He had been waiting patiently below the

little wooden gallery for some time when Bab appeared. He knew her ways. She would come out to the spring by the corner of the house for water, or to close the old green window shutters, or to stand and look at the sky and breathe the fresh sea-air for a few minutes, as was her wont during the indoor evenings she bore so badly. Hartas did not dare, now or ever, to do anything but wait quite silently; and he had been waiting for more than an hour when at last he heard the click of the wooden latch. Barbara came out, stood at the top of the five little steps, listening, as it were. How was it that she seemed to know so quickly that someone was there, that that someone was Hartas Theyn? She certainly could not see him in the dim light that was where he stood.

'It's late for you to be so far fra Garlaff,' she said, coming to the edge of the little wooden platform and bending over. Hartas could see her now in the light from the window, and he could hear her voice, the unencouraging tone of it, the absence of all welcome in it, of all pleasure. And yet what was the meaning of that slight difficulty that seemed almost like tremulousness for the moment? Hartas was perplexed.

'It's none so late,' he replied, putting much emotion into the quiet emotionless words, and drawing nearer to the gallery as he spoke. 'It's none so late. Why there's lights all over the place yet.'

'The lights i' the windows o' fashionable folk,' Bab replied, with unaccustomed satire. 'They're goin' to bed, worn out wi' lissenin' to the band all the mornin', an' goin' up the cliff side i' the lift to lunch. An' then they get more tired wi' drivin' aboot i' carriages all the afternoon; an' they've got to sit two hours at dinner, an' then there's the band again. Oh, it mun be a wearyin' life, that o' theirs. . . . Yet, after all, I'd like to try it for aboot a fortnight.'

'A fortnight! You'd never stand it that long, Barbara,' Hartas said, speaking in far gentler tones than Bab herself had used. 'But I don't wonder that you should wish for rest, for change of some kind. I often think of you, an' of the way you work, morn, noon, an' night. It would kill most women.'

Barbara laughed, not a pleasant laugh to the ears of Hartas Theyn.

'It 'ud kill some men,' she said, 'it might even do 'em harm to hev to think of it. An' Ah don't wonder at you bein' struck wi' the sight o' work of any kind !'

Then she stopped, and presently added with even more of bitterness in her tone:

'If you've wondered about me, I've wondered about you, an' not a little ! How do you ever get through the days? I should think every day was like a week; an' every week like a year. Oh, me ! I can tell you I hev wondered how you live your life, an' you a man !'

Hartas was blushing under the cover of the night; Bab's too sharp and eager words smote upon his own consciousness of the unworthiness of his existence so that every sentence hurt him like a blow. And yet there was something to be said in answer. Mastering as well as he could the hot tide of anger that was pouring over him, making him quiver to the very lips, he strove to make reply.

'Every word you've said shows how little you know o' the truth,' he began, using more impressiveness in his tones than she had ever heard before. 'I've been idle anuff, most o' my life, I admit that, an' not without regret neither; but there was something to be said for me, if there'd been anybody to say it. I'd no eddication, because when I was a little fellow I didn't want none, an' liked better bein' all day long about the Grange, wi' the men, an' horses, an' cattle. An' instead of anyone forcin' me to go to school, my father was proud o' me, because, bein' so little, I rebelled and wouldn't go. An' they used to set me upon the table, my uncle an' him, an' make me tell folk what I thowt o' the schoolmaster, an' when I said some impident thing, they'd all burst out i' laughter, as if I was the cleverest child i' the world.

'An' then by the time I was older, my father had grown indifferent, an' didn't care how things went, nor what I did, nor what nobody did. All he wanted was to be let alone. An' he dreaded when folks like the Canon or Mrs. Kerne came botherin' about me. An' because I was ignorant an' uncultured, an' couldn't talk to them as an equal, an' felt nought but embarrassment, I grew to hate the sight o' them; an' the hatred was like anger, an' made me insolent. An' all the while I was as miserable as I could be; for the home's miserable anuff, I can tell you, an' always has been. But 'twas never till I'd seen you, Bab, 'at I knew what shame was. Even when you were a little thing toilin' and moilin' on the scaur all day, I'd ha given the world to ha' come an' helped you a bit, as that David Andoe used to do, as he does yet maybe, for aught I know.'

'I'm noan one to need help fra no man,' Barbara said, softened into replying with less of bitterness in her tone. 'An' if all be true as you say, why mebbe one ought to ha' been more sorry nor vexed wi' you. But it's noan over late i' life, it could never be over late to begin to mend.'

'An' that's just what I'm trying to do; what I've been tryin' to do this year past, ever since I came to know more of you and your life. But there's nobody to see any change in me, or if they do see any it's only something to be sneered at, an' there's nought i' the world so bad to bear as a sneer because your tryin' to get yourself out o' the old groove.'

Bab did not reply for a moment or two, then she said eagerly:

'Does your sister sneer at you, the one that lives at the Rectory? Does *she* sneer when she knows you're tryin' to make a new beginnin'?'

Hartas felt his answer too deeply to have it on his tongue very readily.

'*Her* sneer!' he said at last; 'her sneer at anything good! Eh, but the very question shows how little you know her. . . . I don't know much of her myself, an' mebbe I might say " more's the pity " if I knew all it meant. An' it's not her fault 'at we're little more than strangers. I didn't want to know her, or to see her; an' for years I took some pains to let her know that I didn't. An' yet she's never resented it i' no way; mebbe she knows 'at there's things to be said on the other side. They've talked against her at the Grange, and said as how she was " stuck up;" an' of all bad things to bear, that's about the worst to me. An' I believed them; an' when I heard her talk it seemed to me 'at her way o' speakin' was mincin', an' over fine; an' her ways was far o'er fastidious for a rough chap like me. An' at last she was no more to me nor a stranger I'd never heard tell of. . . . But now,' and here Hartas's voice changed and softened—' now it seems as if she'd been carin' all the while, an' feelin' lonely, an' wishin' only as she'd had so much as one real brother or sister i' the world. I'd never dreamed of it, it's all new; an'—well, if the truth must be told, I'm feeling as if there was nought I wouldn't do to please her. No, there's nought but one thing, an' that she'll never ask, no, she'll never ask it, Bab, if you let her know you as *I* know you. She'd never dream o' wishin' anybody to make such a sacrifice o' their whole life as that.'

For a little while Barbara was thoughtful and silent.

'No, your sister would never ask it,' she said, speaking in a low, fervid way, rather as if she spoke to herself for her own strengthening than as one speaking to another. 'She'd noän do that — not of her own free will; but what she'd never ask for one might offer her, mebbe. . . . Or no, it 'ud ha' to be done without words! Anyhow, for *her*, one would do it, an' willingly,—ay, more than willingly.'

# CHAPTER XIV.

## THE STORY OF A MISTAKE.

'And soon we feel the want of one kind heart
To love what's well, and to forgive what's ill
In us—that heart we play for at all risks.'
*Festus*, P. J. BAILEY.

HARTAS quite understood; comprehending not only the meaning of the woman he loved, but the depth of her strong determination. She was capable of this thing that she was evidently revolving in her mind; and the idea thus newly and suddenly presented to him was sufficiently disturbing.

'When have you seen my sister last?' he asked, after a pause which had given him time to view the situation with some dismay.

'This afternoon,' replied Bab without hesitation. 'I'd been over to Danesborough for flithers; and had come back to Ulvstan by the train . . . Miss Theyn was i' the street, in her carriage. She'd her hands full o' roses; an' she gave 'em to me.'

'An' you'd sacrifice, not only yourself but me, because o' that!' Hartas exclaimed, the hastiness in his tone betraying much that the merciful darkness was hiding. But though Bab could not discern the hot tide of colour that had risen to his face, she felt the change in his accents, and was silent.

'Because of a handful o' flowers that never cost her a ha'penny, an' likely anuff was never meant for you, you're willin' to throw me an' all my hopes overboard for ever! . . . Good heavens, what strange sort o' stuff a woman's made of!'

Even as he spoke he remembered the day on the beach, when, for all his natural want of perspicaciousness, he had discovered that his sister had suddenly won more of Bab's favour and affection than he had been able to win by the effort of months, nay, of years. At that moment he had been half-glad, half-proud; but he saw it all in a new light now; and the vision exasperated him, though he could hardly have told whether it was his sister or Barbara Burdas against whom his anger was turned.

He had not been particularly hopeful before; but this new fear seemed to destroy the hope he had had, and to do this with a completeness for which he himself could not have accounted.

'I didn't come down here to hev no words,' he said, remembering sadly enough the loving, longing feeling that had beset him as he walked down from the Grange; a longing to pour out all his heart to Bab; to tell her of his new consciousness of wasted life, of his remorse and repentance, of his only half-comprehended desire for better things. For him, as for most human beings, a true love was proving that it held the key to truer life, to fuller light. He had not attained to anything yet; but knowledge was coming to him hourly, that attainment was not only desirable, not only possible, but imperative, if he would live at all, if he would not remain in that slough wherein he had lain so long. He put it down to the fact of his ignorance that all seemed so obscure, so undefined, that instead of some clear aim and rule to guide him he had only a more or less vague longing for better things—a longing that seemed to be bound up inseparably

with his desire to win the love of Barbara
Burdas.

> 'The cygnet finds the water, but the man
> Is born in ignorance of his element,
> And feels out blind at first, disorganized
> By sin i' the blood—his spirit-insight dulled
> And crossed by his sensations. Presently
> He feels it quicken in the dark sometimes,
> When mark, be reverent, be obedient,
> For such dumb motions of imperfect life
> Are oracles of vital Deity,
> Attesting the hereafter.'

The aspiration which had come to Hartas Theyn did not touch any far-off future; it was held by strong bonds to the disappointing and cruel-seeming present; and out of all his thinking, and feeling, and enduring, hardly anything could be put into words. Bab understood how it was with him; and the long silence did not seem long to her, the torrent of her own thought and emotion was too full and rapid for that, and certainly neither of them dreamed that *another* was impatient of the pause, that *another* listened for the next word — listened breathlessly and eagerly. Having hitherto caught only the tones of the speakers, and perceiving that these did not betoken the friendliness of feeling believed on the Forecliff to exist between Barbara Burdas and the Squire's son, it was no wonder that Nan Tyas should be drawn by an irresistible curiosity to listen. Nan was not at any time what might be called an over-scrupulous woman. Though she had now been married some six months, she was still little more than a girl; and being David Andoe's sister she had especial reasons for wishing to know the truth.

She was not a loving woman. Passion, of various kinds, she might already be acquainted with, but the gentleness of true affection was as strange and unaccustomed to her as to any of her ungentle family. Yet she had some liking for her brother David, a liking made up of regard for his forbearance, of respect for his indomitable high principle, for his unswerving effort after a perfectly patient endurance of trials which she but half understood to be trying at all. She knew, as she could not fail to do, of his unhappy love for Barbara Burdas, and in this matter her sympathy, if indeed 'sympathy' her fierce and narrow feeling could be called, was all for him.

To-night accident had led her round by old

Ephraim's cottage, or the 'Sagged Hoose,'* as
it was called upon the Forecliff, from the fact
of its having suffered so severely in a landslip
as to have lost all claim to perpendicularity.
Strangers looked upon it with amazement
when they knew that it was inhabited by a
family of respectable fisher-folk. But Nan
was not thinking of the house, or of its
crookedness, as she went rapidly by the path
from the Andoes' home to her own, a path that
led behind the Sagged House, and away across
the waste sea-front of the rock to her own
cottage on the southern side. It was late,
half-past ten at least; and though Nan was
alone she had no expectation of anything
happening, least of all anything that would
enable her to carry a word of comfort to her
brother David.

Nan was already weary of standing there by
the tarred paling that ran along the edge of

---

\* Sagged (according to Robinson's Yorkshire 'Glossary')
means 'bulged out at the side, as a bowing wall.' But the
word is used in other ways. For instance, a woman's gown,
drawn at the seams, will be said to 'sag.' So, too, Shake-
speare in *Macbeth* v. iii. :—

> 'The heart I bear
> Shall never sag with doubt.'

what had once been a stone-quarry, and was just above old Ephraim's cottage. She knew that the Squire's son was still there; she could discern the outline of his figure as he leaned upon a solitary gate-post, from which the gate had gone long ago. Barbara, being on the little wooden gallery, was out of sight, though not out of hearing.

'I didn't come down to hev no words,' Hartas had said at last, speaking with much more of sullen anger in his tone than was in his heart.

Bab, feeling sorry for him, and being in pain and perplexity for herself, made no reply.

Naturally the mind of each had wandered far enough from the point touched at that moment; still Hartas seemed as if he would take up the conversation where it had been left off.

'No; I didn't come down here to quarrel,' he said, in gentler and truer tones. (Nan Tyas could distinguish every syllable.) 'I came for a purpose very different fra that, Barbara; an' I can't go no roundabout way to it neither. . . . You know what it is! If

I've never asked you the same question in plain words before, I've all but done it many a time, when you've stopped me, either by one means or another; an' I must ask it now. An' I'll say the truth as to what I believe. I don't think 'at you care so much for me, not yet; but I do think 'at you'll come to care, if you'll let me hev the chance o' winnin' you. Hev I made a mistake, Bab, i' thinkin' 'at you don't allus look at me so coldly now as you used to do? I've fancied so sometimes lately; an' I've been that glad when you seemed to give me a kinder look 'at I've hardly known whether I were walkin' on the ground or on the air. It's none my way to talk wild, as you know; or I'd say things stronger nor that. Mebbe I may say 'em yet if you give me the answer I want. . . . Bab, you will say it? You'll be my wife? I know you will! You'll never cut a fellow off frev all the hope he hes i' the world? An' you shan't repent; no, never for a moment so long as you live, if I can help it.'

Still there was silence.

Barbara's heart was beating with such wildness as it had perhaps never known before;

and the tears would have come but for the strong forcefulness exerted to keep them back. Never yet, never for one moment, had temptation been so strong; never before had it seemed so light a matter that Miss Theyn should some day blush for *her* ignorance, that Miss Theyn's kind eyes should droop in sorrow because of *her* awkwardness, *her* ill-bred ungraciousness. This was the sole hindrance on the surface of her thought; but there was more below, much that she only half comprehended. What was it, that something that spoke of some light to be had, some good to be gained, some platform to be reached, the lower step of which might be reached by even a gatherer from the limpet rocks? The one thing that was clear to her in this perplexing moment was that she must at least wait, that she must not obey the longing—it was pressing upon her somewhat heavily to-night—the longing to lay down her life's hard burden, and rest upon the deep and true affection offered to her. Bab did not doubt its truth.

If she had spoken openly, she would have said:

'I do love you, even now; and my love for

you is sweet to me; yours for me is comforting —sustaining. Love is more than all I had dreamed or imagined. But something within me is incredulous of so great a good, and will not let me accept it.'

It even seemed as if in this strong and strange contest Bab's courage was giving way —the one great quality which had seemed to place her so high above her fellows, leaving her timid and helpless as women are supposed always to be. And inevitably Hartas Theyn discerned the fact. We hide nothing from each other. Dissimulation at its best is never more than a partial success.

'You've no answer, Bab?' he asked, with tender surprise in his tone; but intense feeling was underneath.

For all his fever of anxiety he could yet be glad that no quick and emphatic denial had swept his hope to the ground.

At last Barbara spoke.

'No,' she said. And Hartas knew, and Nan Tyas knew, that her voice was the voice of one subduing a very passion of sobs and tears. 'No, I've no answer. . . . That's just the truth—I can't make no answer.'

In one moment, one misguided moment later, Hartas Theyn was beside her on the little wooden gallery, his arm was round her, her face was raised to his, all unawares and against her will. For one not-to-be-forgotten moment, Barbara Burdas was overmastered by the mingled forces of love and strength.

And Nan Tyas knew it all, stooping there in the darkness, bending forward with her ear turned in the direction of the cottage door, and her face hot with the strain of listening. She knew everything.

'I have no answer,' Bab had said.

'Then I'll take an answer!' Hartas Theyn exclaimed in the first flush of his momentary success.

But the next moment Barbara had freed herself with a single strong effort. Standing apart, alone, conscious to her finger-tips of a new shame, a new and unexpected humiliation, speaking louder than before, and far more angrily than she knew:

'*Take* an answer!' she exclaimed. And Hartas Theyn could see the flashing of her eyes in the faint light from the window; he could discern in her tone the surprise and indignation that had come upon her with his ill-judged action. 'You'll *take* an answer!' she repeated. 'Eh, but it's little you know o' me, if you think I'm one to be treated so! . . . No, Mr. Theyn, I'll find an answer noo, since you're so eager for one; an' it's soon said. You asked me to be your wife, an' I say, *No, never!* I'd marry no man 'at showed me so plain he'd no more respect for me nor that! There's my answer! . . . Good-night.'

Nan Tyas heard the quick bolting of the cottage door, the sharp rattle of the window-blind as it dropped over the panes. Then she knew that Hartas Theyn walked away with slow and heavy step and frequent pauses, but not pausing near enough or long enough to hear the sound that Nan heard later—the sound of subdued and bitter weeping.

'She'll noän wed *him*,' Nan said to herself, as she went homeward. 'Her pride 'll never stand such ways as that. There's more nor a chance for David yet; as he shall know afore he's a day older!'

# CHAPTER XV.

## SOME ART CRITICS.

'Humanity is great;
And if I would not rather pore upon
An ounce of ugly, common, human dust,
An artisan's palm, or a peasant's brow,
Unsmooth, ignoble, save to me and God,
Than track old Nilus to his silver roots,
. . . . . Set it down
As weakness—strength by no means.'
E. B. BROWNING.

ALL the morning, since the first ebbing of the tide, Damian Aldenmede had been sitting there under the cliffs beyond Yarva Ness, his easel with its broad canvas before him, a white umbrella behind him, a carefully kept and curiously-set palette, with the usual sheaf of brushes in his hand. A noticeable figure he made in that wide stretch of land and sea. Usually the scene was a more or less dreary one, inclining to a melancholy speculativeness, or to unhopeful acquiescence; but no such mood might beset any responsive human being on a morning so free, so fresh, so blue, so sunny as this. Damian Aldenmede's tall, thin frame was not the home of a soul that could be called unresponsive.

After working with more than his usual rapidity for a couple of hours, putting on canvas, with what truth and poetry of truth were in his power, the great gray nab that ran out from the land, and crossed a considerable stretch of the sea, he was now resting awhile, surveying the result of that long spell of sea-born inspiration. He was not wholly satisfied; what true creator is ever satisfied with his own creation?

In all the Bible is there no more striking and suggestive passage than that one to be read in the Book of Genesis:—'And it repented the Lord that He had made man on the earth; and it grieved Him at His heart.'

This is startling; but it is entirely conceivable; and a man might find motive-power enough for a change of life, were he to try but for one hour to grasp all that that strange and awful repentance must have meant. It must have involved and included so much more than we can even dream of here. The repentance of an All-knowing and *All-foreseeing* God! We imagine it to be contradictory; and so it is to our finite reasoning and understanding. Our utmost effort can bring about no satisfactory reconciliation, and few altogether reverent minds could wish to attempt any such reconcilement. The great hereafter, heaven itself, is made more attractive by the thought of all we have to learn; and if to this you join the added power of learning and discerning that we may hope for, we get a brighter and more living glance and grasp of that eternity which, being in a large sense vague, may not be entirely unappalling to some, and those not the worst, not the most dead to aspiration.

By the ancient Greeks—the worthiest and best of them—the pleasures of the intellect were accounted the highest of all, the pleasures of learning, of knowing, of thinking, of discovering; and this pleasure was inherent, not heightened in any way by the display of

knowledge as an accomplishment. So far as
these authors and thinkers of that olden
time knew they were wise and right; but
the pleasures of the still finer, the still higher
part of man's nature had not then been made
manifest as they were to be made by the
development of a new dispensation. This
higher discerning was reserved for the followers of One despised, rejected, misunderstood in His own day, save by a responsive
few. We, the inheritors of these few, seeing
by their light, discern more clearly the
nature of the most perfect felicity possible
to man, and therefore have keener appetence
for it, keener hope and expectancy. By
this hope we live. The miserable man is he
whose hope is dulled—dulled by care, by
sin, or by neglect of spiritual culture. Does
it need the combined effort of the three to
destroy the soul meant for far other than
destruction? That they run one into another
in ways unexpected, undreamed, we all of
us know; and those who deny most strenuously the existence of any tempting personal
spirit of evil, must yet admit the existence
of some ingenious and most forcible laws of

deterioration. . . . These we do not understand; how should we? But we can at least believe in them sufficiently to dread a time when disbelief may be no longer possible.

It is not the man who, to use an easy saying, is 'born good'—to whom purity and uprightness are as first instincts; it is not this man who can enter fully into the life of him whose soul is weighted from the beginning with strong impulses toward evil that beset him, body and mind. And here is the root of much of our harsh judgment. We see the error, but not the strange and peculiar force of circumstance that led the erring man into sin before he was well aware. We see his fall, but not the long and sore strife with overwhelming temptation.

But while we are thanking God that we are not as this man, it may be that God Himself is stooping from heaven to comfort him with all divine and most efficacious comfort.

'Which of My Saints, of the men possessed by the Prayer-spirit, from Abraham to Gordon, was without spot or stain? Which of them was unblessed by repentance? Was not the oft and grievously erring David a man after My own heart ? Did not Magdalen love the more because there was in her so much to be forgiven ? Is it not an echo, and also a proof of the felicitous bliss of My Divine Forgiveness that there is no finer and more perfect human emotion than that between two loving human souls, one of which receives full forgiveness from the other ?'

So one might hear, if one listened, with other words more consoling still. Damian Aldenmede had heard.

'The upright man is dear to Me,' saith One. 'The man who loves much is dearer yet.'

And there is even another. 'To him that overcometh will I grant to sit with Me in My Throne.'

Him that overcometh ! This is the touchstone. The man whose way is plain, and smooth, and easy ; into whose life no question as to strife, as to yielding, has ever entered ; this man may not be shut out from the kingdom, since such slight test was given him whereby he might prove himself worthy to enter. But not for him the shout that shall go up before the Throne of God as greeting to those who have come out of great tribulation.

'In my Father's house are many mansions.'

You had only to look once into the face of Damian Aldenmede to see that he was now, at least in one sense, like the Master whom he would fain follow, were it but afar off. At the first sight you knew that you looked upon a man over whose head the waves and storms of life had swept pitilessly.

It was a calm enough face now—indeed, the most forcible impression you received was one of a human being, strong and tranquil; and in the same moment you saw that both the strength and the tranquillity were of the kind that come by long and sore strife.

Contradictions were not wanting — they seldom are on the face of man or woman of middle age. The young, who have not entered into the fight, the old, who have fought and won—or lost—these may impress you with unity, with consistency — seldom others.

On this artist's face, for instance, except when in perfect repose, the extreme gravity would be half-betrayed by certain curves that declared him not incapable of humour; and the stern, ascetic lines about the mouth were somewhat neutralised by the tenderness of the deep, sad gray eyes—eyes that were sure to be uplifted to yours, at first with something of inquiry in them, of searching, as if once more he were asking the question:

'Shall one find human faith on this human earth?'

It is Emerson who says:

'I confess to an extreme tenderness of nature on this point. It is almost dangerous to me to "crush the sweet poison of misused wine" of the affections. A new person is to me a great event, and hinders me from sleep.'

Not less keenly had Damian Aldenmede felt on this matter; and, need one say it, all his life he had suffered in proportion to the depth and keenness of his feeling. The assurance most present with him now was that they are happiest who expect least.

In one thing at least he was fortunate, in being able to gratify his instinct for movement whenever the desire came upon him. If he had not wealth, then poverty did not chain him by the feet. If no ties of human love held him by beseeching hands, still he had freedom and power to secure the solitude he had come to prize so greatly. And he was not incapable of weighing, of duly appreciating the good he had.

As he sat there on the point of rock by his easel, looking out over the rippling tide, soothed by its murmuring, soothed yet more by the far stretches of blue sky, of bluer distant sea, the extreme gravity of his face seemed to relax a little; then his head was bent listeningly. By-and-by he smiled, and the austere face became winning, beautiful, pathetic, in the light of one of the most human of human pleasures.

It was only a song that he listened to, a doleful ballad of an older day, sung by girls' voices, that rose and fell upon the breeze, now seeming near, now floating afar. At last the words became plainly discernible:

> 'And tell that ladye of my woe,
>   And tell her of my love;
> And give to her thys golden ring
>   My tender faythe to prove.'

This was only sung by one or two voices; next there came a little chatting and some laughing; then a chorus came that might have been sung by a dozen voices at least:

> 'Yee fayre dames of merrye Englande,
>   Faste youre teares muste poure;
> For manye's the valiante Englishman
>   That yee sall see noe more.'

All the voices joined in this, with some attempt at part-singing—crude, unscientific, yet with a certain most attractively wild sweetness. This was followed by a single voice, young, clear, fresh, as the wind from the sea. Now and then it seemed to vibrate tremblingly, as if to the pathos of the words of the old ballad:

> 'Fayre Alice shee sat her on the grounde,
>   And never a worde shee spake;
> But like the pale image dyd shee looke,
>   For her hearte was nighe to breake.
>
> 'The rose that once soe ting'd her cheeke,
>   Was nowe, alas! noe more;
> But the whiteness of her lillye skin
>   Was fayrer than before.'

By this time the girls had come to the

angle of the rock; there were seven of them, tall, straight, strong-limbed fisher-girls, each with her basket of limpets on her head; each dressed in her own half-masculine, wholly picturesque costume. They made a striking group as they came swiftly onward, with swinging gait, and gay, fearless countenance. Damian Aldenmede, comparatively young though he might be, and certainly strong, was yet half-envious of the quick, vivid, energetic life displayed in every movement made by these fisher-girls of Ulvstan Bight. He had discerned them before they were aware of his presence under the tall, blue-black rock.

It was the white umbrella, the easel with its wide canvas, that attracted their attention first. Then came a momentary pause in the singing, an echo of faint, surprised laughter; but almost immediately the singing was heard again. By this time it was the turn of the soloist, who was no other than Barbara Burdas.

> 'And nowe came horsemen to the towne,
>   That the prynce had sent with speede;
> With tydings to Alice that he dyd live
>   To ease her of her dreade.
>      o      o      o.     o      ♦

> 'But the page hee saw the lovelye Alice
> In a deepe, deepe grave let downe,
> And at her heade a greene turfe ylade,
> And at her feete a stone.'

So Barbara sang, in impressive, thrilling tones, that rose and died away with a plaintiveness that seemed to belong not altogether to the words, nor yet to the quaint and simple music, but to some special quality in the singer's own nature. She came onward, a little in advance of the others, singing as she came, and bearing her burden of limpets—some three stones of them—on her head, with a kind of unconscious consciousness of grace, the grace of strength in her bearing. Damian Aldenmede, watching her, seemed to be almost perplexed in his surprise. The possibilities of form, of action, of attitude, were all awakened in him with that new forcefulness of impression which is so much to an artist. It is in such moments that he lives and moves—moves rapidly onward.

Yet nearer the girls came, smiling archly, singing—

> 'Yee fayre dames of merrye Englande,'

lifting coquettish glances to the face of the artist who sat quietly by his easel, a man too grave, too long and too deeply tried, to be abashed in such a crisis as this. He raised his eyes to meet the eyes of the tall central figure—it was nearer to him than the others—and almost on the instant he became aware that this was not a first meeting. Apparently they were both aware of it.

But the others did not perceive. They were finishing their chorus in a light, easy way. With the last words they stopped by the easel, looked at the artist with eager, interested, surprised looks; then they turned to the nab in the distance, glancing from it to the canvas and back again with the glance supposed to be peculiar to practised and competent judges.

'It's noän sa bad!' said Nan Tyas encouragingly.

' 'Tisn't black anuff,' Marget Scurr interposed.

' It's ower far awaäy,' remarked Nell Furniss.

Still the artist sat there with seeming impassiveness, listening to these untrained, yet perhaps not quite untrue art-critics; but since their remarks were in nowise addressed to him he could hardly make reply. He noticed many things as he sat there; amongst others, that Barbara Burdas had no word to say, critical or other. She was looking at the sketch with eager eyes, with parted lips, and with an air of intense interest, which naturally increased the artist's interest in her. Meantime her companions were moving away, impatient for their noonday cup of tea and freshly-caught herring.

'Ya'll be comin' when yer ready, Bab!' Nan Tyas said, looking back with a meaning, mocking glance, which Bab returned with a steady look of warning. Damian Aldenmede saw and understood. This woman was not to be trifled with, even by her own companions. Her look, the power in it, the unconscious demand of self-respect it betrayed, increased his sudden regard for her, and awoke the desire to know more of her that was later to lead to such unexpected results. How frequently in our life does a look have the dynamic force of an event! No observant human being has lived his life without being aware of the fact that much is said, much done, in which neither word nor action has any part.

# CHAPTER XVI.

### BARBARA BETRAYS HERSELF.

'The effect of the indulgence of this human affection is a certain cordial exhilaration. In poetry and in common speech the emotions of benevolence and complacency which are felt towards others are likened to the material effects of fire, so swift, or much more swift, more active, more cheering, are the fine inward irradiations. From the highest degree of passionate love, to the lowest degree of good-will, they make the sweetness of life.'—EMERSON.

ANOTHER moment or two they stood in silence, then the artist said, with respectful tone and manner:

'Surely I have seen you somewhere before? . . . I have not been here for many years; yet I seem to remember you.'

'Many years!' Barbara replied, looking into the worn, much-enduring face before her, and all unconsciously using a less rude degree of the dialect of her daily life. 'Many years! It's just five this herring-time ... I remember so well. It was the year after the big storm. Mebbe you heard o' that?'

'Yes, indeed; and now I remember. You are Barbara Burdas,' he said, with an increase of gravity, and speaking as much to himself as to Bab. 'And many things come back with my remembrance of that same summer. . . . Yes, many things.'

Then he looked into the girl's face again, the face that had been so beautiful, so touching, five years ago, and now was more beautiful, more touching than ever. He could not but continue to look, to question silently, to answer himself silently also.

'There is trouble there,' he said, discerning by the light of the bygone trouble that was dead, but not buried, in his own heart. . . . 'There is sorrow, and yearning, and strength, and determination. There is no yielding, there is no joy, there is no hope. . . . Poor child! for you are but a child in spite of all contrary seeming.'

All this the artist's eyes said, and Barbara understood in a degree, and her face was slightly averted: she was not used to sympathy and understanding.

'I remember your loss,' the artist said. 'Your great loss! And your grandfather—how is he?'

'He's hearty, thank ya.'

'And the little ones—how many? I forget the number.'

'Four; they are all well, all bonny, all good. Nobbut Jack gives a bit o' bother now an' then; but he's not a bad bairn.'

'Only troublesome? You are right, that doesn't mean badness, very seldom. But about yourself—what have you been doing all these years? Working—that I know; but your life has not been all work, not merely work, that I can see! . . . I can see much, some things that make me sad. Will you forgive me if I speak out—if I say just what I am thinking? . . . I am fearing that you have suffered, that you have some sorrow now—some sorrow of which you do not speak. Am I mistaken? Am I reading your face wrongly?'

Bab blushed deeply and smiled with a very sad sweetness, while the tears that rose to her eyes were dashed away with most impatient gestures.

'It mun be a queer face, I'm thinkin',' she said, with a touch of inevitable satire. 'Or else you mun be one o' the thought-readers 'at one hears tell on i' the newspapers.'

'But *you* don't read the newspapers, Barbara?'

The girl looked up in surprise. The tone of the interlocutor's voice seemed to her to have reproach in it, which she could not understand, yet she must speak out.

'Yes,' she said. 'Every week o' my life I read the *Ulvstan Mercury*—most of it I read aloud to my gran'father—he's despert keen o' the news. I used to be troubled wi' the strange things 'at I didn't understand; an' more especially wi' the strange words 'at I couldn't saäy. But now I can guess sometimes; an' I've begun to see 'at it's all i' eddication, the difference atween folk. If you'd a thousand pounds i' gold, and had no eddication, you'd be nowhere. But the worst o' the newspaper is that there's never anuff about nothing to satisfy ya. There's a little bit o' this, an' a little bit o' that, an' ya're left just about as wise as ya were before.'

The artist was listening keenly, noting sadly. 'You have no books, then?' he asked after a time.

'Oh, yes, ever so many!' said Bab, rather proudly. 'We've the Bible, an' two prayer-books, an' the Methodist Hymn-book. An' then, noän so long ago, Miss Theyn gave me the "Pilgrim's Progress," an' I've read it three times through already. But there's other books I know, a sight o' them, an' I reckon they've all got something in 'em 'at one 'ud be the better for knowing. One sees them i' the shop-winda's. But then, they're not the sort o' books for such as me—very few o' them. They're meant for scholars—for such as——'

Barbara did not finish her sentence, nor did she sigh or look despondent as before. Instead, she merely turned her face and looked out to the sea, out to where the white-sailed ships were gleaming and gliding in the far blue distance.

'You are thinking of some one?' Damian asked gently.

'Yes,' Bab replied, with her usual instinct toward ingenuousness. 'Yes; I was thinking of her—Miss Theyn. You'll know her maybe?'

'No; I do not. I was here a very short time, and I did not then desire to know anyone. . . . Who is Miss Theyn? The Rector's daughter?'

'No; the Rector's niece. Old Squire Theyn's her father; but she lives at the Rectory.'

'And she is a scholar?'

Bab raised her eyes swiftly.

'I should think she is!' was the emphatic reply. 'Eh! you should hear her talk—it's beautiful. The words is like—oh, I don't know what it is I would say! It's just as if one was lissenin' to music.'

'Is this lady young?'

'Yes . . . I think so; but Ah doän't know, for she's sa tall an' sa stately, at times she's even haughty like; but I can't tell hoo it is, ya seem ta love her more for it. Ah'm noän one 'ats given to takkin' nought fra nobody; but there's been times when I've felt 'at I would sooner take a blow frev her than a good word frev anybody else. . . . It is straänge!'

Damian was listening, noting. The girl was rising to eloquence, if not exactly of words, then of tone, of expression. The colour came and went on her face, the fine mouth quivered slightly, the blue eyes sparkled to each fresh thought.

'She is beautiful, this lady, I am sure?' the artist said, not with curiosity in his tone, but musingly, as if he confirmed something to himself.

'Beautiful!' exclaimed Bab, her own face irradiated to a beauty she herself could not have appreciated, even had she seen it. 'Beautiful! Eh, me! Ya should see her when she looks at ya, when she turns her head a little i' talkin', so as to look straight into yer eyes! An' then when she smiles— oh, I could never tell ya! Ya feel as if there's nought i' the world ya wouldn't do for her, an' ya feel dooncast like, an' ever sa far away, because there's nought ya *can* do. I've laid awake o' nights many a time thinkin' whether there wasn't *nought* she'd hev, *nought* I could do. . . . There's the lobsters; they're despert sought after by the better sort o' folk. Ya know the old sayin' aboot Ulvstan lobsters and Flamboro' crabs? Well, but then, you see, so 'twere to be 'at she needed any such thing, she could buy a pot full, an' never miss the money. So where's the good?'

Damian Aldenmede was listening quite gravely, comprehending quite clearly.

'No,' he said, without a shadow of a smile. 'No, I shouldn't think of the lobsters. But needlework, now—something of that sort?'

'Needlework!' poor Bab said sadly. 'I've thought of it; but I'm a despert poor hand. Ah can make a bit o' frock for Ailsie; but it never fits, not rightly. Ah'd no help i' learnin', ya see, my mother bein' gone. An' as for fancy things, such as ya see i' the shops, beautiful silky things, wi' pearls an' velvet, why, a touch o' my hand 'ud drag 'em all to pieces, as if ya swept a ling besom across 'em. No, there's nought Ah can do, not a thing, but stare at her like a fool when Ah see her, an' then go home an' cry fit to burst the heart in my body because Ah can never be nothing to her—nothing at all!'

It would be difficult to describe with any accuracy the impression that Damian was receiving from the fisher-girl's betrayal of the deep affection won by a woman so far above her in all that makes difference in human sight. He would not deliberately have called himself a student of human nature, yet few things deserving notice passed him by unobserved.

One of the many ideas pressing upon him now was this, that here was a woman, young, eager, capable of some culture, yet held by ignorance as some are held by physical blindness. He could see her, as it were, groping for light, patient under the need for it, but with deep sadness lying concealed under the patience. What if he could help a little?'

Not being quite a young man, having drunk somewhat deeper than most men of the cup of experience, he could not all at once give way to the sudden impulse that beset him—an impulse that would have led him to surround this girl with such books as might be useful, and to help her to suitable teaching. He must think of it. Yet he would retain, or rather acquire, the acquaintance needful to the carrying out of his project, if he should decide to continue his intention.

For awhile he had been silent, looking down to the stone-strewn beach at his feet, apparently wondering if this or that pebble were the celebrated 'plum-pudding stone' of Ulvstan Bight. But it was another kind of wondering that really occupied his brain.

It moved him to speech at last.

'Do you work *all* the day?' he asked, 'or is there some definite time set to your working? What, for instance, do you usually do in the mornings from ten to one?'

Bab smiled thoughtfully.

'Ah do a deal i' that time, most days,' she replied. 'But the worst's over afore one o'clock. As a rule, we're at the flither-beds by four these light mornin's—that is, when the tide fits.'

'And the flither-beds are two miles away?'

'Nearer three.'

'And you come back about this time?'

'It's accordin' to the tide. We'll be late this week, an' most o' next.'

'I see! Then if I were to ask you to be kind enough to stand or sit for me, whilst I make a picture, a likeness of you, it could only be in the afternoon?'

'Only i' the afternoon these tides,' said Bab, again blushing deeply.

'And you have no objection? You would oblige me by coming, by remaining in the same position here on the rocks for an hour or more at a time? . . . I do not, of course, wish you to give me your time without adequate return.'

Did Bab understand this 'art of putting things'? Damian was not sure. The girl looked into his face half-wonderingly. Then she said, in her simple, straightforward, yet not undignified manner:

'I'd like to come. . . . I like to lissen to ya when ya speak. . . . Can I come to-morrow? What time will ya want me? Two o'clock, will I saäy?'

## CHAPTER XVII.

### A REVELATION.

'Oh what a power hath white simplicity!'

ALMOST as a matter of course, Barbara had told her grandfather of her interview with the gentleman down on the rocks by the ness. Old Ephraim listened silently, smoking his pipe, looking up somewhat curiously into Bab's face.

At last he spoke.

'Thoo mun mak' a bargain wiv him, Bab!' he said, slowly and emphatically. 'Deän't thoo goä wastin' thy tahme for nowt. They can afford it, them artises. Why, oäd Tommy Battensby tell'd me wiv his oän tongue 'at yon man 'at painted sa mony pictures o' t' wathermill up aboon Garlaff had meäde a thoosan' pun oot o' that bit o' beck alleän—a thoosan' pun i' less nor fower year! Think on't! Think o' that noo, an' deän't thoo be ower eäger-like. Haud off a bit, an' he'll come doon—niver fear!'

Poor Bab! She hardly knew why this speech jarred upon her — why everything seemed to be jarring just now. She said but little in reply to the old man's characteristic warnings and exhortations. He had never before seemed to her to be selfish or grasping. Now, though they were quite alone, the idea of 'making a bargain' with the kindly and understanding stranger caused the colour to rise to her face for very pain. Already she had been thinking in a vague way that if he should ask her to accept money she would not take it. Other girls on the Forecliff had taken payment for the same service, she knew; and they had boasted of it afterward; and Barbara had felt herself to shrink from self-comparison with these. Now she shrank more than ever, since coarse handling had made her feel as if the transaction itself would have a certain coarseness in it; and a sting was already in the pleasure that was to have been so pure and so welcome.

Nevertheless, she went down to the rocks the next day; and Damian Aldenmede saw with something that was almost distress that she had brushed her luxuriantly-straying auburn hair until it was as nearly smooth as it could be made to lie, that she had discarded her red shawl and her blue guernsey for a badly-fitting lilac-print gown and a clean white apron. The change was as a complete transfiguration.

'Who shall say that dress goes for nothing after this?' he exclaimed inwardly. Outwardly he was as much at a loss to know what to say as if he had been dealing with a duchess.

But Bab saw instantly that something was wrong. Was it little Ailsie's presence? Bab had brought her sister down with her, thinking that she might cover any awkward moment that might occur; and also because she was never so happy as when the child was by her side.

She was a winning little thing, as Damian saw at once, despite the Sunday frock and the hideously-shaped hat of white straw, with its grass-green feather. Bab had daringly gone to the best milliner's shop in the town to buy the hat, knowing that she would have to pay for her temerity; but she had not grudged her hard-earned money, since little Ailsie was so pleased and had kissed her so warmly. It had made chatter for a week on the Forecliff; but nowhere had it created the impression it was creating now. The artist was in despair, for the little one's face grew upon him with every glance he gave. It was so soft, so sweet, so pure, so touching, that he resolved at once to paint the sisters together if he might. The contrast between Bab's largely-moulded figure, her handsome features, her air of independence, and the gentle, wistful, delicate appearance of the seven years' old child at her feet, was too striking to be foregone. He would make an effort, a desperate effort if need were.

There had been a moment of awkwardness, of silence, of mutual disappointment, which Barbara did not at all understand. At last the artist spoke:

'I ought to have told you,' he began, speaking in a kindly regretful way—'I ought to have said that I wanted you to come just as you were yesterday, without your bonnet, and wearing your work-day dress, as I wear mine,' he added, glancing at his suit of gray tweed. 'And the little one—don't be offended with me, but she is lovely; and if I might paint her too, I should be more grateful to you than I can say just now. . . . You are not angry?'

The latter question came because of the change that the artist saw on Bab's face—the tide of hot colour, the quivering of eyelids over eyes, that seemed as if they might fill with tears on ever so little more provocation.

'Angry? No,' she said, restraining herself by a great effort; 'but when I thought I'd done everything I could to please you, it's——'

'It seems a little hard,' said the artist, speaking so gently and sympathetically that Bab could not but perceive that he knew all about it. And as a glimmering of the true state of affairs began to dawn upon her mind, the tendency to tears became a tendency to smile; and the artist smiled too; and little Ailsie laughed a soft low laugh that drew all attention to herself.

'Then what will we do?' said Bab, quite herself again, and having a generous twinkle of humour in her glance, that proved her quickness in passing from one extreme to the other. 'What will we do? Come down again to-morrow afternoon, me wi' my creel on my head, an' Ailsie wiv a string o' dabs in her hand? How would that be like suitin' ya?'

'It would suit me to a T,' replied Damian, entering into Bab's new mood all the more gladly because of the moment of pained constraint. He could not help adding, 'How quick you are to see!'

'D'ya think so? D'ya think that truly?' Bab asked, with sudden glad earnestness.

'Certainly I do, or I should not have said it.'

Bab did not ask the next question that was trembling on her lips. Instead, she paused, and looked out, as her frequent way was, over the peaceful sea, that seemed so wide, so suggestive of things not to be reached or touched, yet always to be desired.

'Ya really meant that?' she said, looking into the grave face before her with a wistful, eager, pathetic look that marked the relationship between herself and little Ailsie. 'Ya mean it—that I am not sa stupid?

'You stupid? By no means!' was the emphatic reply. 'What could make you think that?'

'Everything,' said Bab decidedly. 'I know nothing, not as *they* know. I can't even speak as they speak. An' if I were even to *try* down here, there'd be nought but laughin' an' jeerin'. Oh, it's hard—harder than you think!'

Again the artist was silent, impressed by the fervour of the girl's manner; discerning that there was more below the surface than he could expect to arrive at all at once. Surely there must be something beyond mere admiration for the Rector's niece underneath all this fervidness, all this strong desire! And then, quite suddenly, he recollected that he might have known the truth—perhaps more than the truth, if he had not, somewhat peremptorily, closed the lips of his too-loquacious landlady on the previous evening. Now he had to bear the result of his want of knowledge.

'I think I can understand,' he said presently, putting down his brushes and palette, and seating himself upon a big, brown, tangle-covered stone. He had previously offered his camp-stool to Ailsie, who sat perched upon it with the prettiest ease of manner and bearing; her little brown legs crossed, her clumsily-clad feet swaying down below. Overhead the tall cliffs were towering darkly; the gulls were screaming and chuckling in and out.

'I think I can understand,' he went on. 'I can remember the time, though it seems long enough ago, when nothing seemed to me so precious as knowledge. And—don't answer me unless you like—is it *that* that is troubling you, that you have not what the world calls education? Is it *that* you are desiring so much—for its own sake?'

He might well ask the question. For the most part, those who do so desire it are the last to dream of external help. They have helped themselves, unknowingly, unconsciously, long before they were aware of what they were doing; and there is no crisis of their life wherein they awaken to demand of others some aid in taking the first step. But though Barbara Burdas was not of these, her desire was not the less real.

She listened to what Damian Aldenmede was saying wonderingly; her face was bent downward, her forehead drawn into lines by the weight of the thought presented to her.

'For its oän sake,' she murmured presently. Then she lifted her troubled eyes to the artist's face, and continued, 'Hoo can one tell? Would I ha' cared if it hadn't been for *him*? Would I ha' cared at all?'

Damian could only look at the girl with inquiring looks. She comprehended the inquiry, and an expression of pain came over her face.

'Ya don't know! How should ya? Yet I thought ya *might* have heard, sin' it's all over the place. . . . It's him; her brother, as I told you of yesterday. . . . But, oh me! what am I saying? He's nought to me—no more than the wind that blows. . . . What is it in ya that makes me talk o' things that never was, nor never can be? . . . What have I said? There's nought in it—no, nought at all!'

'You are speaking of the brother of the lady you mentioned yesterday—Miss Theyn. Do you know him? Do you know him intimately?'

'I know anuff' about him—more nor anuff',' Bab replied. Then, instantly remembering herself, regretting her words, she said, speaking more sadly, 'All I've got to do wiv him now is to forget him—to forget I ever set my eyes on him, or ever opened my lips to speak to him, or ever let my ears listen to a word he'd got to say.'

Damian Aldenmede was not blind, nor altogether shortsighted. It was but natural that he should construe for himself the words he had heard; and his own past experience led him to an almost dangerous verge of sympathy.

'I think I know all you would wish me to know,' he replied; 'and I see that you are distrusting yourself—your own wish for something more than the mere production of a daily tale of bricks. Yet why should you—especially since you are so sure that you have no other wish, no other hope? And yet I think I understand you, the doubt you are in; and, if I may advise you, I should say, put all doubt aside, and trust your higher instinct. I speak to you out of my own past experience when I urge you to set your mind on the attainment of something outside yourself.'

'Some knowledge, ya mean—some larning? I'm thinkin' on it always, night an' day.'

'Then no greater earthly gift could have been given to you than a desire like that. I know what I am saying. I have tried to influence others to the same end; but I have failed for the most part because I could not put into other minds, other hearts, *the spring* that moves my own—the *mainspring of desire*. . . . This great blessing you possess, however you may have come by it, I perceive that you have it; and to any man who can see as I see, who is looking out over the dreary waste of human life as I am looking to discern one human soul like yours, truly hungering and thirsting for something more than mere bread and shelter, is, believe me, to see a sight to encourage one—to make one glad. Nothing could give me greater pleasure than to be allowed to help you. It would take the dreariness from my evenings while I am here as few other things could do. Please say that you consent.'

Bab was watching him, gravely, wonderingly. There was a quiver at the corner of her mouth — a light in her blue earnest eyes.

'Do I take ya rightly?' she said, speaking as if with difficulty. 'You would be willin' to larn me something yoursel'?'

'Yes—more than merely willing.'

'An' ya think I *could* larn?'

'I am quite sure of it; quite sure that you could learn everything that it is necessary for you to know.'

Bab remained silent, and Damian turned away, searching among the pebbles at his feet for the belemnites so frequently found on the beach at Ulvstan. He would give her time to think of his proposal.

But by-and-by he was startled by the sound of a sob; one deep, half-restrained burst of emotion. He turned to where the girl was standing, little Ailsie by her side. The child was clinging to her, lifting a pale beseeching face.

'Doän't cry, Barbie; don't cry! What's he done to ya? What's he said?'

'It's noän *him* 'at's made me cry, honey,' Bab answered, taking the little one in her arms, kissing her to hide her own emotion. 'It's noän him! . . . He's kind an' good; an' we mun be kind to him if we can. But we can't; that's the worst of bein' poor. There's nought you can do for nobody to show 'em how ya care.'

'There are various ways of showing,' said the artist. 'And since you feel that you would be glad to do some good turn for me, please believe I am equally glad to do something for you. But we mustn't stop at words; and since I may not stay here very long, we must waste no time. How much time can you give me? A very clever man once said that an hour a day, regularly given, would enable a student to climb almost any particular mountain of knowledge he might wish to climb. Can you give me that—a whole hour daily?'

'Ay, an' more,' replied Bab eagerly, wiping some tears away with the corner of her apron. 'There's four-an'-twenty hours in a daäy;

an' I'm never i' bed more nor five on 'em. . . . But you've yer oän work to think on.'

'So I have; but I seldom work more than four hours a day. My eyes grow less sensitive to colour after that; and for conscience' sake I desist. So don't think of me. I have idle time enough—time that I shall be glad to spend in a manner that will bring me more gratification than all the art-work I shall accomplish in my lifetime.'

'Doesn't yer work give ya no pleasure?'

'It doesn't give me the pleasure I long for, the pleasure of being in any sense satisfied with what I do.'

'Still ya go on trying?'

'Always trying, always hoping.'

'Then mebbe ya'll come to it at last! . . . I hope ya will, for you've been sa good to me.'

'You will let me be good? You will let me come in the evenings for an hour, shall I say seven to eight? Would that be a suitable time?'

'It would be suitable anuff,' said Bab, again changing colour, and speaking with some indecision. 'But couldn't I spare you the trouble o' comin'? Couldn't I come to Mrs. Featherstone's?'

'No,' the artist replied. 'It would be better that I should come to your grandfather's house. Is he at home in the evenings?'

'Yes: allus. But he'd not be i' the waüy. He smokes his pipe, an' dozes till bedtime without much talkin'.'

'Then I'll come to-night, if I may. And you will forgive me for the mistake of this morning?'

Bab smiled,—not the scornful smile she was so apt to use.

'Forgive!' she said. 'Ay, an' forget an' all.'

'You won't forget to come down to the rocks again to-morrow?'

'No,—an' I'll not forget 'at you like us best i' the every-daüy wear. . . . Come, Ailsie! Saüy good-bye to the gentleman. We mun be goin' home. Gran'father 'll be wantin' his tea badly!'

## CHAPTER XVIII.

### AT ORMSTON MAGNA.

> ' To man propose this test—
> Thy body at its best,
> How far can that project thy soul on its lone way ?'
> ROBERT BROWNING.

It is strange how, in some lives—lives that seem fair, pure, peaceful—any true, and high, and perfectly spiritual aspiration is yet a rare thing. The outside world looks on, seeing a man or woman whose life is without spot or stain; whose name is on every list of names charitable; whose place in church is never empty; whose whole demeanour tells of a careful walk, with uprightness in every sense of the term. And that outside world is not mistaken; it seldom is. Hypocrisy may remain practically undetected; it never passes altogether without suspicion.

And yet even that outwardly stainless, and inwardly true human being may be aware of a lowness, a deadness, that is almost as bad to bear as any consciousness of actual sin could be. Thorhilda Theyn was a woman of too high nature to permit of much deadness of spirit without self-protest. Hitherto her inner life had consisted largely of a kind of mild warfare, with more of compromise in it than she cared to perceive except on the occasions when she was compelled to be honest with her own soul. And these were perturbed times; for she did not spare herself. Any other person, knowing her whole life, would have set down much to the exaggeration natural to an imaginative woman.

The heart knows its own bitterness, and the soul knows its own failure; and few could have felt more acutely than did Miss Theyn that her life was below her own highest standard.

And she had no real excuse—this she knew.

'I have no cares,' she had admitted to herself; 'my mind is not distracted by the need of fighting for bread. I have no doubts;

God has mercifully given me a soul, a mind, that can accept His every saying without question. I have *no* hindrances to bar me from the spiritual life, none but such as are within myself, *growing, increasing* within myself!

'*I am too much at ease!* Trouble might stir me; and yet, how I shrink from it, even from the idea of it!

'If I had to live Gertrude's life, for instance, I think I should not care for another year of existence. These surroundings are so much to me; the ease, the comfort, the never having to move from my sofa or easy-chair, not so much as to write a note unless it is one I wish to write; the warmth and softness of everything, the very fire in my bedroom night and morning for nine months of the year; the fact of having a carriage at command morn, noon, and night; the knowledge that no wish of mine for food or dress, or for any of the little luxuries of daily life, is ever disregarded or forgotten, all these things are as the air I breathe. I have never once thought of them definitely till now; but now I know that I could not exist without them.

I fear that the smallest deprivation would be intolerable.'

All these things Miss Theyn had admitted to herself, and not without self-blame, on the evening before the garden-party at Ormston Magna. The party of the year it was to be, so everybody was saying; and Thorhilda was not without suspicion that it was being given with a definite end in view, an end that concerned herself. She would be made to perceive more clearly than ever before Percival Meredith's ability to gather about him, in his own home, whatever of rank or fashion the neighbourhood contained.

There were several county families within a certain radius of miles. Lord Hermeston, of Hermeston Peel, had accepted the invitation. Lady Thelton and her four honourable daughters were coming. Sir Robert and Lady Sinnington were expected; with squires and dames of all degrees; and people not distinguished in any particular way had been invited in numbers sufficient to almost fill the terraces and gardens of Ormston.

Both Canon Godfrey and his wife were of opinion that the day was meant to have a special influence upon their niece's decision; and Mrs. Godfrey did not for a moment doubt what that decision would be. From the first she had thrown all the weight of her own conviction into the scale on the side of the owner of Ormston; and believed that she had not done so in vain, but her husband had very greatly questioned as to whether the matter was so entirely a foregone conclusion as Mrs. Godfrey appeared to think.

It would soon be seen, however. The eventful day—a day in early August—broke brightly upon the earth. Not a cloud threatened. The far, still sea was shining, studded with the silvery rippling lights that seem to glitter like stars upon a sapphire floor.

All the morning Thorhilda walked about the Rectory gardens, an unread book in her hand; cool, sweet-scented airs upon her forehead; perturbing thoughts in her heart—so perturbing they were that she was glad to see Gertrude Douglas come smiling down between the standard roses, the great blue larkspurs, and the golden lilies.

Gertrude was beautifully dressed in primrose cashmere and purple plush. Even Miss

They did not know that the costume was a present from her Aunt Milicent to Miss Douglas. Mrs. Godfrey was not a woman who liked to do such things as that with ostentation.

'Let it be between ourselves, dear,' she had said to Gertrude. 'For after all it is a selfish sort of gift. I do so like to see my friends well-dressed. And Thorhilda really cares so very little that I often feel quite troubled.'

That had all been said a fortnight ago; but Miss Douglas had not forgotten it. She came gliding down to the west arbour, conscious of beauty, of a certain indefinable fascination which was neither of the heart nor of the intellect, and yet had force to impress others. There were moments when Thorhilda half-resented an impressiveness which she could not comprehend.

'Not dressed yet! Why, *my dear!*' Miss Douglas exclaimed in her high-pitched, yet most musical voice, coming forward to bestow an eager kiss as she spoke. 'What time do we start? Four! Isn't that late considering the length of the drive? And, why, what's the matter? You look quite doleful! And on this day of all days of the year! Well, you *do* surprise me! If such a party had been given in *my* honour, I should have been dressed hours beforehand, and rehearsing my part in a darkened room, so as to concentrate all my faculties.'

Thorhilda returned her friend's kiss with a certain emphatic quietness; and not wishing to discuss the matter alluded to, she did not disclaim Gertrude's idea as to the intention of the gathering at Ormston Magna.

'A rehearsal in a darkened room?' she said, by way of reply. 'That *does* remind me of poor Aunt Averil, who, for years past, has tried to induce me to give an hour a day to the study of manners. She has a little morocco-bound book, with tinted paper and gilt title, in which she has written an entire code of good manners, with extracts from every book she has ever read bearing at all upon the subject. A fresh acquisition is read out to me each time I go to the Grange. The time before last it was a quotation from "Lothair," to the effect that *repose* was of the essence of beauty; I forget the exact words. Last time the quotation was from Lord Lytton, and urged the larger duty of trying to enter into other people's views, other people's ways of thinking. It was something like this:

' " Few there were for whom Harley L'Estrange had not appropriate attraction. Distinguished reputation as soldier and scholar for the grave; whim and pleasantry for the gay; novelty for the sated; and for more vulgar natures was he not Lord L'Estrange?" '

'And your Aunt Averil keeps a book of that kind?' said Miss Douglas, with such regard in her mention as she had never shown toward Miss Chalgrove before. 'I do hope she will leave it to you.'

Thorhilda could not help the smile that came—a smile of many meanings. In reply, she said:

'I told Uncle Hugh of our conversation when I came home. He, too, was amused at first. Then he opened a New Testament that was lying near, and for a little while he seemed to be reading, or thinking. Then it was as if he spoke to himself rather than to me; his utterance was disjointed, like one speaking in his sleep:

'"There is nothing new under the sun," he said, rising from his chair and walking to and fro slowly in the dim light that was at the farther end of the drawing-room; his hands, still holding the Testament, were crossed behind him, his head was bowed thoughtfully, his voice came sweet and pure and earnest.

'"No, there is nothing new," he continued. "The finest refinement of manners cannot go beyond St. Paul—except in one direction only—the manners of his Master. But to remain below these, on the merest human level, has it not all been said, all that your essayists and novelists and poetical critics of life can bring forward as to the essence of the matter? You are not to think of, you are *to sacrifice self?*—that was said long ago! You are to be all things to all men! St. Paul said, 'I made myself a servant unto all!'"

'And then he went much further, into greater and finer detail. "Only for a moment," he said—"just for one moment, change St. Paul's word '*charity*,' and substitute 'fine manners!'

'"Fine manners are kind; they envy not, they vaunt not; those who have them are not puffed up.

'"Fine manners behave in no unseemly way; the man who is happy enough to possess them does not seek his own. He is not easily provoked. He is not capable of thinking evil.

'"He rejoices not in iniquity—no, nor even in hearing of it. His greatest joy is to hear of the good and the true.

'"Moreover, the man of fine manners can bear all his sorrows, his trials, in the dignity of silence. If even he should have to bear upon his heart and brain the weight of the wrong-doing of others, he can yet bear without complaint.

'"And the secret of all this is simple in the extreme. 'He believes all things.' Believing, he can endure in calmness, in joy.

'"And yet another event, his fine manners 'never fail.' Other things may fail, and cease, and vanish away; but the man or woman who shall use as his or her pocket-book of etiquette the thirteenth chapter of the First Corinthians shall not be found wanting.

'"The man or woman nurtured, trained on the teaching of the New Testament alone, shall be at a loss in no good society. The rules are there; the disposition to obey the rules is innate. The lowest saint, the humblest follower of Jesus, shall shine in the highest human society that this or any other land can produce."'

So the Canon had spoken one evening, not long before the eventful day to be recorded. And Thorhilda reproduced his words as closely as her memory permitted. Becoming aware that her complacent friend was growing restless, she desisted.

After all the preparations that had been made, it was yet late when the Rectory party started — four of them in Mrs. Godfrey's pretty light brougham, the remainder in the waggonette. On arriving they saw at once that the lawns and seaward terraces were filled with guests. A band was playing in the shadow of the north end of the house; tennis-courts had been marked; a long white tent sheltered the refreshments that were being dispensed by numerous servants, male and female. In the paddock, on the southward side of the house, targets had been set up for archery; but since the Market Yarburgh club was of recent date, no one expected much entertainment from the efforts of its members—and, indeed, just now it was too hot for exertion of any kind. Mrs. Meredith came forward to greet the Rectory party under the shelter of a rose-pink parasol; her son Percival was by her side, ready to take Thorhilda's hand as she stepped from the carriage, and yet not forgetful of Mrs. Godfrey or Miss Douglas. No one could find a flaw in his courtesy, now or ever; but he at once made it evident to everyone that his especial attention that day was to be devoted to Miss Theyn. He had reason enough for being proud of his position. He remained by her side as she shook hands with this group of distinguished guests, and with that, and his approbation of her graceful, reserved courteousness increased at every step. He noted her perfect ease of manner, her unconscious dignity, her rare and exquisite loveliness, with all the pride of one anticipating the further pride of possession. All through the afternoon he remained near her, moving with her through the gay crowd, sitting a little apart with her under the shade of the wide beech-trees listening to the band, watching the tennis-players, pointing out to her his rarest and most perfect flowers, waiting upon her lightest word, and doing all with the quiet, eager intention that alone might have betrayed how it was with him. People looked at each other with the look of half-amused intelligence natural at such times; some whispered, some even ventured on a question to Mrs. Meredith, whose pretty gray silk dress seemed to be shining everywhere.

'Is it all fixed? Mayn't we know?' asked Lady Thelton, who was the most intimate of the friends present at Ormston.

But Mrs. Meredith put up her little white hand deprecatingly.

'Oh, hush!' she said. 'I am superstitious. I never talk of a thing until it is beyond the possibility of failure.'

'*You* superstitious!' laughed Lady Thelton.

'Oh, my dear, what will you accuse yourself of next? But I see; I am to be discreet! Well, give me time to think of a wedding-present worth sending.'

Was Thorhilda conscious of all the wonderings, the surmisings that were going on about her? She hardly knew. She seemed to herself to be more perturbed than happy; more bewildered than content. And yet as the hours went on, swiftly, dreamily, she knew that she was yielding, yielding half against her wish to the overpowering influence of the emotion that was subduing another so completely that its force, like an electric touch, was communicated to herself. Outwardly as calm, as strong, as dignified as ever, inwardly she felt helpless; and she could make no protest when she knew that she was being gradually and designedly separated from the crowd — drawn by a glance, or less, to a solitary nook between the hillsides, and beyond the gardens, a copse filled with a tangled undergrowth, through which a little beck went trickling and singing down to the sea. Before she knew it, they were alone— she and Percival Meredith; alone and silent

—so silent that the note of a bird seemed loud and intrusive, and the gurgling of the water some want of deference on nature's part. For a long while there was no other sound.

# CHAPTER XIX.

### UNDER THE LARCHES.

> 'A vague unrest
> And a nameless longing filled her breast—
> A wish that she hardly dared to own,
> For something better than she had known.'
> — J. G. WHITTIER.

PERCIVAL MEREDITH was a man who had sufficient assurance for all the ordinary purposes of life, but he was well enough aware that the present moment was in no sense an ordinary one. Yet he wondered a little at the strength of the emotion that was besetting him; it was new and strange. Though he had known love before, or something that he had counted for love, he had never till now felt this almost hesitancy that held him in its grasp. It was not till he had made the effort of recalling the facts that Mrs. Godfrey had given him all the encouragement that a woman in her position could give; that the Canon had shown him a kindly welcome at all times, whilst Miss Theyn herself had never exhibited the faintest distaste, or seemed other than pleased by his presence—it was not till he had recollected these things with some vigour that he began to regain the standpoint natural to him. Even now it was not easy, and Thorhilda was not making anything easier for him.

She stood leaning against the trunk of a young larch-tree, straight and white and still, even a little sad now, if her expression were any true index of her feeling, and yet to Percival Meredith's thinking she had never looked more beautiful. Her white cashmere dress fell into graceful folds, and mingled with soft, creamy lace and loopings and floatings of ribbon and borderings of plush. The only ornament she wore was a Niphetos rose, which he himself had gathered for her and given to her earlier in the afternoon.

'It was good of you to wear my rose,' he said at last, speaking in a low voice, and lifting his long dark eyelashes in a certain languid yet effective way peculiarly his own. Thorhilda blushed under his gaze, but faintly, and with as much consciousness of disturbance as of pleasure, yet the beautiful soft, sea-shell pink made her seem lovelier than ever in his sight, and, half unconsciously, he drew a little nearer to her side.

'But all you do is good and kind,' he continued. 'It is that gives me hope, and that only. Though I have watched you, tried to make myself something to you, some part of your life, these two years past, I must admit that I have yet no assurance. One moment, nay, perhaps for a whole evening, I have felt more or less happy, because I fancied you had given me more or less ground for hoping that you were beginning to care for me. Then, perhaps the very next evening, you have taken the ground from under my feet. Can you wonder that I have often known something like despair? That for a long time past I have felt as if I *must* know what the end was to be—whether I was to hope for a whole long life of happiness, or for a life of something more nearly like misery than I dared to think . . . . Lately the suspense has been growing terribly. Can you not imagine it?

Can you not sympathize with it—at least so far as to say that I may hope that you will soon put an end to it—the end I yearn for? . . . You can never, never destroy my one earthly hope!'

While Percival was speaking, naturally enough Thorhilda was thinking, thinking rapidly, feeling intensely, as people do when the heart and brain are raised to their highest and swiftest power by the rush of the fresh force of life through vein and nerve. And here she found the good of much previous right thought, high desire, and frequent prayer. Even in this impetuous moment she said to herself, 'I cannot have lived under the same roof with my uncle Hugh for nothing, and surely now, if ever, I must strive to see the right. . . . Would that I had openly asked him about this before, talked it over with him! . . . I must do it, I must do it yet before I give any definite answer. . . . Yes, I must request time for that!'

Not once did it occur to her—how should it, in her youth, her inexperience of love, life, all things?—that a perfect affection, perfect within itself, would have needed no outward constraint, no external drawing or pressure, no help of any kind.

But meantime, while she was thinking, Percival Meredith was moved to pouring out a very rhapsody of loving, pleading words, less preconsidered than those he had used before. Thorhilda had not dreamed that he could be so eloquent, so impressive, so fervent! It was her perception of this latter quality that drew her to be real also.

'I did not know, indeed I did not, that you cared for me so much,' Thorhilda replied with timid simplicity, trembling, blushing, feeling so faint under the weight of new and strong emotion, that she longed to lean upon the strength of the man who seemed so all-sufficient for her support, then and after. What was it restrained her? She could not do it. Despite her weakness, her almost yearning and tender weakness, she shrank from self-betrayal. 'I cannot answer,' she said at last. 'I cannot give you any answer now!'

She stopped. Percival took her hand, holding it gently, as one who would quiet the fear betrayed. It was some time before he began to plead again.

'*Not one word?*' he said at last, '*not one single word?* It is all I ask. . . . And, no, I will not ask even that, if it is to cost you so much. How could I ask anything from you but that you should not forbid me to wait? I will wait as long as you wish, only do not say that I may not hope. At least, at the very least, say that I may hope that you will be good to me some day! . . . I wish you knew how I long to be *something* to you, to be in a position to—to save you from anything that might happen in the future. . . . And—and we none of us know!'

Thorhilda was only half-aware of the sudden restraint that came over Percival Meredith. Of the reason for it, for the sudden drooping of the eyes, the unexpected failure of the words of the man she was, or seemed to be, on the verge of loving with her whole life's love, she knew nothing.

How should she know? There had been whispers abroad of the Canon's unrestrained and unconsidered generosity; of family claims, the claims of younger brothers, with their wives and little ones; poor, unenterprising, clamorous; but of all this Thorhilda had known nothing; and therefore had thought nothing. Once or twice it had struck her as a little strange that her Aunt Milicent should seem to be so emphatically on the side of early marriages. 'I might have thought she wished me to leave her,' Thorhilda had said to herself more than once in moments of perplexity; but no such ungracious and ungrateful ideas had remained with her permanently. And no thought of this kind had any weight with her now. She was only conscious of a strong desire to avoid the utterance of anything that should seem to be binding upon her afterward.

And yet, even in this troubled moment, she felt that she must some time yield. Half she feared that she would do this, and half she hoped that she might be compelled by some circumstance outside herself to do it.

But even now she did not recognise the fact that no hesitation ought to have been possible to her—no, not for a moment. A true and healthy human love knows no more of hesitation as to whether it shall betray itself, than a healthy human life knows of hesitation as to whether it shall go on living. If a test were wanting, here is one ready-made for most uses.

But Miss Theyn was fully conscious of her perplexity; and, as was natural to her upright spirit, she confessed it.

'I cannot, I cannot understand it,' Percival Meredith said in reply; speaking with a new and moving humility, that was yet not untempered with self-respect. 'I cannot understand. You either care for me, or you do not! . . . Yet forgive me! As I said just now, I am most willing to wait, only, only tell me why I must wait? Will you not tell me that?'

A moment Thorhilda was silent. Then all at once, as it were, her spirit broke from the bewilderment that had held her as in a trance all the afternoon. She lifted her face, raised her beautiful gray eyes, which were deeply charged with all earnestness, all sincerity.

'I will answer you plainly,' she said, speaking with far less of trepidation in her manner than she felt within herself. 'I will tell you the truth so far as I can. And the first thing I must say is that I have no doubt of your affection for me. . . '

'Then thank you for that, a thousand times thank you!' Percival broke in with fervidness, and raising Thorhilda's hand to his lips gracefully as he spoke. 'Again and again I thank you for your faith in me. . . . But having admitted so much, what can hinder you now? Not your want of love for me. Once more I say that I will wait for that. I will try to win that! With all my heart I will try! . . . And what is there beside?—nothing, surely nothing.'

What was there in all this ready protestation that seemed, if not unreal, yet still in some curious way unsatisfactory? Was it the way of men? of lovers? The inquiries that Thorhilda put to herself were utterly childlike in their ignorance, their confusion. She had had no lover before, nor any dream of love. How should she know?

Yet she replied gravely, and with an altogether womanly dignity.

'There is much beside,' she said, and then there was a pause while she made an effort to continue. 'If I am sure of you, or of your affection rather, I am not sure of myself, not in any way. *I am fearing myself; my own integrity;* and I think that you should know of this!'

'*Your* integrity — *yours!*' exclaimed Percival, feeling at least as much surprised as he seemed. 'What *can* you mean? I should as soon doubt the integrity of an angel from heaven.'

'I mean this,' Thorhilda said, her breath coming and going heavily, her eyes set with a seeming hardness in the expression of them, as if the effort after a perfect straightforwardness were testing her strength to the utmost limit. 'I mean this, that I am not sure that I return your affection, or that I ever can return it as it should be returned. I fear much that I never can. And, let me speak the truth in all sincerity, I *know* that I am tempted by your position, by the prospect you have to offer me — the prospect of ease, of wealth, of unlimited luxury for all my future life. I have been used to these things, though they are not mine by birthright; and now it seems to me that I could not well live without them. . . . And, as I fancied you suggested just now, I may not be able to live at the Rectory always. . . . And there is nowhere else — nowhere,'

The silence, the utter silence that followed, was not one to be forgotten. For some moments Percival Meredith could make no reply; and yet he hardly knew what it was that hindered him so powerfully, so completely.

In his own heart he had long ago admitted to himself that in all probability worldly considerations would have some influence with Miss Theyn, more with her friends; and the idea had not hurt him grievously.

Now he was conscious of pain, of disappointment, of disillusionment; and though he could not analyse his feeling, he was aware that he stood as one watching the visible shattering of some idol he had set up to worship; and being not greatly given to such worshipping, the loss seemed all the greater.

Miss Theyn began to perceive in a slight degree.

'I have grieved you,' she said sorrowfully, gently. 'Forgive me. I thought it better to be honest, quite honest.'

'Yes,' Percival replied musingly. 'Yes, perhaps it was. And yet, I wish you had spared me!'

Again there was silence. Somewhere beyond the distant purple of the tree-tops the sun was sinking to the moor; twilight was stealing into the hollow; the rippling of the streamlet seemed to sink to a sadder, a less living tone.

'Let us forget this,' Percival said at last. 'You have not said that you could not care for me; and I think you will learn to care at least for my kindness, my love—the rest will come. I do hope and believe that it will come. I trust the future.'

'The rest!' It had never been so near coming as it was at that moment. Percival Meredith, a little saddened, a little unhopeful, and subdued to a new humility, was very different from the self-assured man who had put aside every thought of failure, and had not been able, for all his diplomacy, to quite hide the fact that he had done so. Now he had nothing to hide; and it may have been that one more kindly and earnest appeal would have been answered to his wish. But that appeal was not made; and it may be admitted that there was reason enough why it should not. He was hurt, and reasonably, and one sign of it was the touch of petulance about his small, restrained mouth ; another sign was the want of perseverance at the one significant moment.

'I will go on hoping,' he said, turning to go, and cleaving a way through the briars for Miss Theyn to pass. 'And you will be good to me ; say that you will ?'

Thorhilda smiled.

'Haven't I always been good ?' she said, holding out her hand timidly, half reluctantly.

'Yes ; indeed you have !' Percival replied. 'As I said before, that was the only excuse I had for my presumption.'

# CHAPTER XX.

### THE CANON AND HIS NIECE.

*'To thine own self be true;
And it shall follow, as the night the day,
Thou canst not then be false to any man.'*

Miss Theyn was not quite happy that evening —how should she be? She was confused herself; circumstance was confusing; and there seemed no light—no help anywhere. On the way home from Ormston Magna, Gertrude Douglas indulged in a little mild badinage, which was quickly repressed. The Canon was thoughtful, absorbed. When Mrs. Godfrey came to know, from the lips of Percival Meredith himself, that Thorhilda's answer had been vague, and not altogether encouraging, an unusual but most visible flush of anger mounted to her forehead, and remained there. Thorhilda saw and understood; and having hitherto seen so little of any unquiet side there might be to her aunt's character, the sight added to her perplexity.

It was some time before the two women spoke to each other of the great event of the day; and then nothing passed that was helpful in any way. Mrs. Godfrey knew more than Thorhilda knew of the reasons why Percival Meredith's offer should have been graciously accepted, and she was too much a woman of the world not to prize to the uttermost the advantages that Thorda seemed quite willing, and quite unthinkingly, to forego for very indifference. This was how the matter seemed to the Canon's wife; the Canon himself saw much farther.

'Surely you would not force her inclination in any way?' he had said, after listening to the torrent of words his wife had poured out in his ear while they were dressing for dinner, the door between their rooms being open for this especial purpose; and Mrs. Godfrey's reply was one that he could only meet with a pained silence. Yet he was by no means insensible to the worldly advantages offered to his niece—nay, for reasons known in all their seriousness only to himself, he would have been at least as glad as his wife had been if Thorhilda had chosen to accept without demur the offer of the owner of Ormston Magna. Yet that she should be even by one word *persuaded*, was repugnant to every notion of honour that he had.

Later in the evening, seizing a brief opportunity, he could not but speak to the girl, whose white, and lovely, and lonely face seemed to be appealing to all the tenderness, all the manliness he had in his soul.

'Tell me about it, Thorda,' he said, laying a gentle kindly hand upon his niece's shoulder as she sat musing sadly by the drawing-room fire. Mrs. Godfrey had retired early, being wearied with the inquietude of her own spirit, and of the day's event. 'Tell me about it,' he said. 'I know the outside facts. You could not say "Yes," not conscientiously.'

'No, I could not,' Thorhilda said, letting a single sob escape in spite of all repression. A weaker woman as much perturbed, as much excited, would have answered with a burst of tears. 'No; that is just it. But to tell the truth I can hardly say where the conscientiousness lies. I am afraid of being dishonest —dishonest toward him or with myself.'

'You have never at any time felt that your mind was made up at all on this matter?'

'No; not for more than five minutes together. . . . Shall I tell you the truth, Uncle Hugh—*all* the truth ? I should like to be mistress of Ormston Magna—I should like it much. In one sense it seems the very place in the world made for me to fill.'

'That is just how it has seemed to me,' replied the Canon. 'You have every quality that would be required—every grace. . . . And I had hoped long ago that it might come to pass. But my hope has limitations. Now, tell me the rest !'

'There is no rest! I like Mr. Meredith, as you know; but not, I think, with the liking I ought to have before I can accept the position he wishes me to fill. . . . He says that this is but natural; but just what he expected; and that all the rest will come. It is here that my trouble lies. As you know, I have hardly known—hardly ever seen anyone else. And at one time I am drawn to him; at another time almost repelled, without any reason for either. . . . I *cannot* understand!'

The Canon was watching, listening; his inmost heart was lifted up for the One light, the One strength, the One guidance that could come to him.

'Have you no word for me, Uncle Hugh—no help?' And as Thorhilda spoke she laid her white, beseeching hand gently upon his arm. 'I am no heroine,' she said. 'I want to do right, but I have not even self-knowledge enough to enable me to know what *is* right. Can't you help me? . . . I have never needed help so much before.'

The unintended touch of pathos in her voice moved the Canon greatly. He turned to Thorhilda with all the warmth of one to whom the unrealized idea of fatherhood was inexpressibly dear.

'I will help you all I can,' he said soothingly. 'I have been blind myself—at least it seems so to me now. And let me say, whilst I have opportunity, that I have not done all for you that I should have done. I could not. I had other claims, hidden from the world's sight, for the most part, but binding to the uttermost. Your claim was binding also; I knew that all the while. I am realizing it rather bitterly now. And it may be too late; I cannot tell! And I fear—I fear much that I counted on your making such a marriage as would quiet all my care for you, at once and for ever. Therefore you see how it is that I cannot urge you to think more favourably of Percival Meredith than your own inclination moves you to do. Under other circumstances I might have pointed out to you much that is good in him, and also the possibility of your influence heightening the good qualities he already has. As matters stand I cannot do this—not without suspecting myself. And, indeed, at present I can advise nothing but waiting—prayerful waiting. . . . Try that, Thorda, dear—*prayer*. There is no other help for this human world. And when light comes, *be true to it!* That is all that I can say. Be true to the light given, wherever it may lead!'

# CHAPTER XXI.

## THAT WAS THE DAY WE LOVED, THE DAY WE MET.

'The love which soonest responds to love—even what we call "love-at-first-sight"—is the surest love; and for this reason—that it does not depend upon any one merit or quality, but embraces in its view the whole being. That is the love which is likely to last—incomprehensible, indefinable, unarguable-about.'—SIR ARTHUR HELPS: *Brevia*.

THERE was no one to counsel, to strengthen Barbara Burdas. If she stood up straight and strong, she stood somewhat apart from those who surrounded her more immediately. And it said as much for their human insight as for her tact that no one seemed to resent her position. If any did a kindly thing for her, the doer knew certainly that in his or her place Bab would have done as much or more.

It is so that many of us accept kindnesses which unsupported pride might rise up to reject. We take them as they are meant, knowing that our own meaning would have led us to the same outward expression. 'You shall do this for me if you will, because in your position I should have wished to do the same for you.' So we reply to ourselves when a false dignity with all its suspiciousness would spoil the moment.

All her life Bab's place among her fellows had been an easy one. She had been admired without jealousy, commended without bitterness, respected without undertone of detraction. Even when her pride, her independence offended, her large kindliness of heart made quick atonement.

So it was that no one resented the fact that she had been chosen by the artist to be the principal figure of his great picture, 'The Resting-place of the Flither-pickers.' Bab was to be in the foregound, just rising up from a brief rest, her basket of limpets on her head, Ailsie clinging by her side, and bearing her little basketful of bait. Half-a-dozen others were to be seated upon the rocks and stones of the mid-distance.

Miss Theyn had heard of the picture,

though, as a rule, she heard little of anything concerning the fisher-folk of the Bight. She might have known quite as much of their innermost life had she lived at York or at Lancaster. It is the stranger who is curious and interested where the resident is indifferent and supine.

It was on the morrow after that unsatisfactory hour at Ormston Magna that Miss Theyn went down to Ulvstan to do some shopping for Mrs. Godfrey, and to make one or two calls in her aunt's name on some of the more prominent parishioners. At Mrs. Squire's, the milliner's shop, she had been so unfortunate as to meet her Aunt Katherine, and though this was only for one moment, Mrs. Kerne had seized the opportunity of making the moment as bitter as might be. Thorhilda bore the small unmerited sneers with outward calmness, but with more of inward irritation than she was accustomed to feel—an irritation that added to the things she was already bearing. When the morning's work was done she dismissed the carriage. 'Wait for me at the Cross Roads,' she said to Woodward. 'I shall not be long.' Then turning down the steep street that led to the beach and to the Forecliff, she half-admitted to herself that she was in search of some distraction that had no name.

'Where am I going, and why?' she asked vaguely, not demanding any answer from herself. It seemed as if the blueness of the sapphire sea alone had power to urge her onward, as if the soothing sound of the wavelets falling and breaking upon the beach alone could impel her to watch, to listen, to pause upon the brink of that river of life upon which she stood. She seemed to be filled with a strange hopefulness as she went onward over the beach, threading her way daintily among the tangle-covered stones on either hand. As she went onward, the sea-breezes blowing upon her face, the shrill cry of the gulls in her ear, she seemed to lose the tremulous sense of the painfulness of human life that had held her so strongly before. A new warmth grew about her heart, a new peacefulness, which made all the future seem plain and easy. Mere physical movement seemed a delightful and pleasant thing.

Was it the sunshine that inspired her and

allured her? She went slowly by the edge of the wavelets that rounded the sparkling sea, which was retreating for awhile from the Bight of Ulvstan, moving gracefully, as to some rhythm, unheard and unknown. By-and-by it would advance again to the singing of the morning stars, joining its music to theirs, helping to complete the cosmic harmony.

Thorhilda's mood was quiet and sweet, yet there was yearning in it; and the smile that was on her face as she rounded the point of Yarva Ness might certainly have been counted a smile of expectancy. She was looking out dreamily, half unconsciously, as people sometimes do who walk alone, and then, quite suddenly, she became aware that she was not alone. There was a large white umbrella, an easel, a wide canvas; an artist with a big gray felt sombrero was bending over a palette, over a sheaf of brushes, making rapid touches, as he glanced to where Barbara Burdas stood, with little Ailsie beside her, among the weed-hung boulders of the Bight. Beyond were the tall cliffs, half hidden by the yellow sunshiny mist, that made the scene like the coast-line of some dreamland or wonderland. Miss Theyn saw none of these details definitely as she went onward with a smile toward Barbara, who stood there, tall, beautiful, almost as dignified as Miss Theyn herself. For a moment she forgot all about the artist, and lifted her creel from her head, without dreaming that the slight action was one to move him almost to despair. Yet he stood by with grave face and courteous attitude, wondering what his next duty might be. He was not so free from perturbation as he seemed. He had forgotten Bab's description, his own anticipation, yet all at once he knew himself to be possessed by that flash of feeling which arouses most of us when at last we stand in the presence of a long felt-after ideal. Here at last is the beauty we have tried to grasp in visions, here is the goodness, here the grace of soul. Being thus prepared we fall down and worship, and are at once the better for that worship.

Rudel knew when the pilgrims brought from the East the accounts of the grace, the loveliness, the goodness of the Lady of Tripoli. He listened till he lost himself, lost himself utterly in the hope to find another. But the story of the troubadour having been told already it may not be repeated here. Browning's brief poem contains the essence of the drama, its most vital human meaning. The man heard and loved, loved so intensely that when the moment came when sight was to be vouchsafed to him his strength was not sufficient for the ordeal; it had been consumed by thought, lit by a supreme imagination. He fell at the feet of the woman whom he had loved unseen, and he died there. Ever since men have sneered at his name, or have grown sadder on hearing it. A few men, a few women, have understood.

Damian Aldenmede had not the poem in remembrance at the moment when he turned to meet the diffident, almost timid glance of the lady of whom he had heard so much. Bab, in her own informal yet unembarrassed way, was introducing this new Lady of Tripoli or of Ulvstan. What's in a name? The Rudel of the hour stood holding his brushes and palette in one hand, raising his gray felt hat with the other, lifting a grave, unsmiling, austere face, with far-seeing eyes, that seemed so full of sadness, of some old hopelessness, that Miss Theyn's one impression was that of a man acquainted with sorrow, and with little beside. Later she knew more, and judged far otherwise.

She was the first to speak.

'I fear I have interrupted you,' she said, in sweet, musical, yet most unaffected tones. 'I ought not to have stopped, but I could hardly help it.'

As she ended her speech she glanced first at the canvas, then at Bab, with undisguised admiration. Bab was listening to her, wondering how her words, her voice, her grace, her beauty would strike this most perceptive artist, who was now disclaiming all idea of being interrupted.

'It is good to have a brief rest sometimes,' he was saying. 'And I am proud that my picture tempted you to stay and look at it. I only wish that it had been in a more attractive stage.'

'To me it is very attractive,' Miss Theyn replied eagerly. 'I have not seen an unfinished picture half-a-dozen times in my life. . . . I find great charm about a canvas only half-covered.'

'Do you paint yourself?'

'No, I regret to say. I learnt to draw, as people do learn for whom drawing is classed with crewel work. My governess taught me. I did a drawing every month, the usual chalk trees, the usual chalk figures, with the usual river impeded by large stones. The only variation was in the ruins, sometimes it was a ruined castle, sometimes a church, sometimes a mill. There was a trick of touch for each.'

'And you learnt the receipt by heart?'

'I learnt it thoroughly. When I had done so I laid down my porte-crayon for ever.'

'Surely not? . . . It is not too late to make up for lost time.'

Bab, who was listening closely, and with intense interest, was not aware of the quiet smile that was creeping unnoticed over her own face.

'Is he always wantin' to learn somebody something?' she asked herself. And truth to say she had hit rather cleverly upon one of the singularities of his character. It was not that he liked teaching in itself, nay, it would hardly be too much to say that he hated it; yet the pleasure of knowing that he had satisfied another's craving for knowledge, or even for mere information, was one of the most satisfactory pleasures remaining to him in life.

Not that he was dreaming of offering lessons in drawing to Miss Theyn; nor had Thorhilda's vision progressed so far as yet. Still she was silent for a moment, and during that moment she was thinking of the possibility of taking up an art that would require time, labour and earnest thought. Then her future, as it had been placed before her only yesterday, rose up all at once, making her feel as one awaking from a pleasant dream to the dull and chill reality of daily life. The smile seemed to die from her lips and from her eyes. Damian Aldenmede, watching her closely, eagerly, saw, and . . . grievously misunderstood.

'She thinks I am presuming—this dainty lady. . . . I will be mindful ! . . . . She shall think so no more !'

Thorhilda replied at last—speaking in quite another tone.

'I am afraid it is too late,' she said, watching the artist as he began to rearrange his brushes, to replenish his palette from the tubes. She discerned the change in him, the increase of gravity, the power of self-effacement; and above all she saw the loneliness, the true heart-loneliness that has outworn all waiting, all searching, all hoping. Seeing that he was wishful to begin his work again, she said a few more words to Bab, gave a smile and a kiss to Ailsie, and turned to go.

There was no embarrassment visible in her manner as she bowed to the artist, saying gracefully, but not without an undertone of sadness:

'Good-morning, Mr. Aldenmede. Thank you much for letting me see your picture. I am sure it will be a very beautiful one.'

'Will he ask me to come and see it when it is done?' was the question in her own heart.

'Shall I say that I shall be glad if she will come and see it many times before the finishing touch is given?' was the question asked on the other side.

Neither interrogation was uttered aloud, though perhaps the inward thought did not stray so very wildly. Miss Theyn went back over the beach alone, perhaps sadder than before, and with a strange and utterly unaccountable sadness. Yet she felt as if all at once a new restfulness had overshadowed her.

'How quiet he makes one feel!' she said to herself, speaking as she might have spoken of one whom she had known for years. 'Is it the strength in him? the goodness? I am sure he is good; and I am sure that he is strong. . . . There is nothing frivolous there! nothing selfish, nothing idle, nothing that could even tolerate luxuriousness.' . . . Then there was a pause—a graver moment. 'And there is nothing that could savour for one second of secrecy, of duplicity. If he is reserved, it is with the reserve of one who would hide from the world's eyes a sorrow that the world could never understand. . . . If I had a trouble, I could tell it to him; he would comprehend, he would alleviate it somehow. . . . I wish, I wish he had not been —what he is!'

Even in thought Miss Theyn could not put any words to her vague ideas of this stranger's poverty; she shrank from her own notion, and felt curiously perplexed. That one who had a more true distinction of manner, a more perfect grace of address, a finer reticence in speech and demeanour than she had ever seen before—that such a one should be lodging at Mrs. Featherstone's, a small, tidy cottage at the back of the Forecliff; that he should seem to be dependent upon his brush; that he should have come into the neighbourhood of the east of North Yorkshire without credentials of any kind, was assuredly bewildering. Yet Miss Theyn's utmost vision did not pass beyond his own presentment of himself. 'Yet I wish—I wish he had been different,' she repeated half audibly. 'I know no one whom I should be so glad to have as a friend. All my life I shall think of him as the one man between whom and myself there might have been a perfect friendship.'

Meanwhile the artist had resumed his

painting with redoubled vigour—working rapidly, silently, eagerly; and Bab saw by the compression about his mouth that he was in no mood for conversation. It was not till he had flung down his brushes and palette and patted Ailsie on the cheek, with thanks for being so still, giving her a bright new florin for her very own, that Bab dared to speak.

There was a touch of humour in her blue eyes when she raised them.

'Noo—did Ah tell ya wrong?' she asked, speaking gently and smiling softly. 'Did Ah saiiy a word overmuch? Have ya ever in yer whole life seen a lady *half* so beautiful?'

Aldenmede did not reply for a moment. Then, laying his hand gently on little Ailsie's shoulder, and turning to Bab with his kindliest voice and accent, he said, using much emphasis:

'Don't misunderstand me, Barbara—indeed, I feel sure that you will not! . . . But how shall I say it? how shall I express what I am thinking—that it will be better that . . . better if you do not speak to me of Miss Theyn any more.'

Bab's only answer was a quick, curious, wondering look. As she went homeward, she smiled to herself, saying :

'He'll speak of her to me afore I'll speak of her to him! But he'll do that, an' afore long, or my naäme's noän Barbara Burdas.'

## CHAPTER XXII.

### IN YARVA WYKE.

'And we entreat Thee, that all men whom Thou
Hast gifted with great minds may love Thee well,
And praise Thee for their powers, and use them most
Humbly and holily, and, lever-like,
Act but in lifting up the mass of mind
About them.'

      P. J. BAILEY : *Festus.*

THE summer was passing on—a bright beautiful summer it was, with now and then a summer storm by way of variation, tossing up the white waves into Ulvstan Bight, scattering the herring-fleet north and south; now and then a sea-fret, chilling yet stifling, defrauding the sight as with a temporary blindness. Yet the actors in the drama of life, as life was displayed on the stage of Ulvstan Bight, went on playing their parts all the same, apparently heedless of storm or shine. Some were bearing patiently, suffering silently; some now and then flew out into mad street brawls, subsiding afterward to hide their misery, cowering by fires of shipwreck wood, seeming to cease from emotion altogether, and only to cling in a dumb brute-like way to the mere fact of existence.

Canon Godfrey, going in and out amongst them, was touched afresh each day by the endurance he saw. Misery was accepted as a natural thing, as natural as labour or pain; and oft he marvelled to see how such as were suffering most seemed best to bear the contrast that was daily increasing before their eyes.

It was in the early autumn that the richer people came to Ulvstan, the people who brought their own carriages, their own men-servants and maid-servants. The resources of the neighbourhood were taxed to provide for their wants, or what were counted as wants; the little shops grew quite enterprising in their efforts; the scene on the beach grew daily more and more gay. Ladies on horse-back came galloping up and down by the rippling tide; invalids in chairs and carriages were drawn to and fro more slowly; little brown-holland children with pails and spades went paddling in and out of pools and sand-castles; crimson parasols burned in the yellow sunshine; pink dresses and blue, white dresses and red, went flitting about among the bathing-machines; and the fisher-folk looked on, and wondered, and did little kindnesses whenever opportunity came in their way with a curious and not unbeautiful acceptance of the inevitable.

'Good God! that one can bear to see it all, and to think of it!' the Canon said to himself one morning, as he walked with his wife in search of Thorhilda, who had gone toward the Forecliff with a basket of flowers for Barbara Burdas, and had not returned to the place where they had expected her.

She had meant to leave them at the Sagged House; but she had found the door locked; and Nan Tyas, passing by at the moment, had stopped to say:

'Is it Bab ya're wantin'? She's noïn i' the hoose; she seldom is at this time o' daäy.'

There was a pertness in Nan's manner, as

she leaned over the gate and lifted her bold black eyes, that aroused within the Rector's niece a touch of something that was almost indignation.

'Thank you!' Miss Theyn replied. 'Perhaps you know where I may find her?'

'Perhaps!' Nan admitted, evidently resenting the momentary haughtiness her own manner had awakened. 'Perhaps Ah do! Ah'm noän boun' te saäy, sa far as I understand the law o' the land!'

Thorhilda's first impulse was to pass onward, without so much as a civil word of departure; but she had force enough to recover herself. Turning to Nan, who still stood with her elbow upon the gate-post and an unpleasant smile upon her lip, she said quietly, and with dignity:

'Has it so happened that I have offended you in some way? Have I been so unfortunate as to displease you, to cross your will or wish in any direction? Pardon my questions; but you seem to speak as if you had some reason for wishing not to oblige me.'

Nan stared for a moment into the pale,

gentle, yet resolute face before her. The kindly expression answering her own insolent one was puzzling. Nan could not resent it.

'Ah doän't know as *you've* ever vexed me,' she said, averting her face slightly, partly in embarrassment, partly in shame. 'But if Ah *mun* tell the truth, you're near anuff akin te them 'at hes.'

Miss Theyn began to understand; and in spite of effort after self-control the understanding brought a flush of pain to her cheek.

'I am not quite sure that I know what you mean,' she replied, speaking in changed tones, yet still with a kindly and winning courtesy. 'You will know that I cannot speak to you of—of others. . . . If you cannot tell me where Barbara is, I will say "Good-morning."'

'Good-morning,' Nan retorted, lifting herself from the gate-post and moving away. But she turned again quickly, Miss Theyn's word and tone constraining her. 'Ah meant noä offence,' she said, 'an' mebbe Ah'd better gie ya a word o' warnin'. They mean mischief—some o' Dave's mates. . . . But, there, Ah can saiiy no more.'

'Stay a moment!' Miss Theyn entreated. 'Mischief, you say? To whom? Not to Barbara—surely not to her?'

'To Bab? Noä, niver! They'll noän harm her! But there's others—there's one ya know, not so far away by kin. Give him a word. If he's not a fool, he'll take it.'

'You are meaning my brother?'

'Ah niver naämed no naämes,' Nan replied, half-tremulously, and again turning to depart. 'It's well anuff known i' the Bight 'at Dave's heart's been set upon her for years past; an' there's noän but what thinks she'd ha' given in sooner or later if nobody else had come between. An' they know how it is! They can see that his heart's just breakin'; and hers is noän so much at rest. They can see it all; an' they've said . . . But, oh me! What am Ah doin'? They'd murder me—toss me over the cliff-edge as soon as look at me if they knew Ah'd betrayed 'em! Eh, me, I *is* a fool! . . . But you'll noän let on, Miss Theyn?'

'Can you not trust me?' Thorhilda asked, her face alight with gratitude, with sympathy, with kindness.

'Trust *you?* Ay, to the death! But let ma go noo. Ah darn't stay no longer.'

Miss Theyn was left standing there by the steps of the Sagged House, perplexed, wondering, irresolute. Then all at once her mind was made up. She would find Barbara first, and then go on at once to Garlaff. Doubtless the fisher-girl would be on the Scaur somewhere—in all probability at the point beyond Yarva Ness where the artist was at work upon his picture. Miss Theyn could see the white umbrella gleaming even from the Forecliff; and at once she began to make her way thither, though not without some reluctance—a reluctance she herself could hardly understand.

She had not seen the artist since that day when Bab had, in her own simple and unembarrassed way, introduced him to her. More than once her uncle had seen him at church, and subsequently had called upon him at his lodging; and unfortunately the call had been returned one afternoon when the whole of the Rectory party had gone to Danesborough. Naturally, a stranger of such distinguished presence and bearing had been discussed at the house on the hill at Yarburgh.

'We must see him somehow,' Mrs. Godfrey had said one evening, not thinking how and where they were to meet.

It was Barbara who was the first to discern Miss Theyn's approach. She was standing in the usual position some two or three yards away from the artist, her creel on her head, little Ailsie by her side. Mr. Aldenmede saw by the sudden change on her face that some one was coming—some one in whom his model was interested.

'Who is it?' he said, smiling. 'Miss Theyn?'

Bab looked at him, and only the word 'roguish' could perfectly describe the meaning of her glance.

'Ah thought that were a name 'at had been forbidden to be said,' she remarked, her expression saving her speech from all touch of temper.

The artist looked up with quick appreciation. There was no time for words. Miss

Theyn's step was upon the gravel behind him. He rose and bowed. Bab saw his colour change, and the carnation that was on Miss Theyn's face deepened to an almost painful degree. The words of greeting were curiously confused.

Thorhilda offered the basket of flowers to Barbara — rich and rare roses, heliotrope, stephanotis, sweet verbena, half-buried in daintiest ferns. Bab took them with an emotion that betrayed to each of the onlookers that her soul's sensitiveness to beauty was not to be measured by any of the outward circumstances of her life. She turned away, silent, tremulous, to hide the basket from the sun within the cave close at hand.

Miss Theyn was looking at the picture; Damian Aldenmede was explaining his further intention concerning it; while little Ailsie was resting on his campstool, her small hand clasped in his. The artist knew himself to have already a singular affection for this tiny child of seven, and that she responded to it helped to fill the lonely days with a quite new and felicitous warmth. He was glad that she was there while Miss Theyn was speaking.

'Have you not been working very hard?' she asked, looking at his canvas, upon which the figures were growing—coming to a fuller life, a finer beauty, a truer human expressiveness. Her question sounded common-place; her well-meant grain the veriest chaff; yet no other word would come.

The artist smiled in answer. Then he said:

'That is true in one sense, yet one never counts the work *hard* that is done *con amore*. The hardness would be in being deprived of the opportunity of working. I do not think that in the intellectual life of man there can be a greater trial than to know that you have something to say or do, and to learn by sad and sore experience that the opportunity of uttering your word or doing your deed is to be for ever denied you.' Then the man's voice changed, faltered a little as he continued: 'If there be a true taking up of a bitter cross it is known to the man who must do some lower work while his whole soul is drawn to live and to toil on greater heights. And it is a trial that not one human being in a thousand can comprehend; therefore the man who suffers it can have no sympathy, hope for none. In the beginning he yearns for it, throwing out feelers here and there, as if searching after response, comprehension; but by-and-by, borne down by sheer disappointment, he ceases to expect these things, and schools himself to a life of silent uncomprehended negation, knowing that he does this to his own loss, perhaps to the world's loss also. Everything has its price.'

Had the man forgotten himself? All at once he seemed to wake up.

'I beg your pardon!' he said emphatically. 'I fear I was not thinking!'

But he saw that Miss Theyn was thinking as she stood there silent, impressed, beside his picture, looking into it with quite new vision. Bab was coming back from the cool cave where she had left her flowers, something glittering among the petals that was not the morning dew. She was by Ailsie's side again, the little one was lifting her disengaged hand to Bab, Miss Theyn was smiling at the evidence of affection that was between the two, when all at once everybody became aware of a figure, leaping, sliding, gliding, making for himself a pathway down the pathless cliff but just beyond Yarva Ness.

Involuntarily the artist was drawn to look at Miss Theyn. She was pallid, trembling, distressed.

'It is Hartas, my brother,' she said; then she turned aside. If some madness were moving him to self-destruction she would not look on while the deed was being done.

# CHAPTER XXIII.

### CANON GODFREY AND HIS NEPHEW.

"For worse than being fool'd
Of others, is to fool one's self."
TENNYSON: *Gareth and Lynette.*

It seemed like a miracle that Hartas Theyn should make that perilous descent, and yet touch the beach unhurt. Thorhilda, turning to meet him, saw that he was white and rigid to the very lips. He looked thinner than he had looked before; and his dark eyes, as he looked from one to another of the little group before him, seemed alight with new and strange fires. So impressive his unexpected presence was that no one spoke for a moment. At last Thorhilda broke the silence:

'This is my brother, Mr. Aldenmede,' she said, making a great effort after self-command. Then, turning to Hartas, she exclaimed: 'How could you do such a thing as that? How *could* you? . . . It seemed impossible that you should ever reach the foot of the cliff alive!'

'There's more than one here that would have been glad anuff if I never had reached it alive!' he replied with ill-controlled emotion. 'But I didn't come down here to talk about myself,' he went on, glancing hurriedly, nervously, to where Bab stood, inwardly perturbed with strange apprehensions, with uncomprehended yearnings, yet outwardly calm, almost dignified. 'I didn't come for *that*,' Hartas was saying. 'I had another erran'— an erran' I'm not ashamed of!'

Then he paused for want of power to continue, rather than for want of words, and Damian Aldenmede, seeing this, came forward with intentions of the kindest.

'Have you known anyone to make that descent before?' he asked, speaking as of a mere question of Alpine climbing, or rather descending. 'Pardon me for saying it, but I think you risked too much. The alum-shale hereabout is like soap — quite as slippery, quite as much to be distrusted for climbing purposes.'

'There's things as is more slippery, more to be distrusted than the alum-shale,' returned the young man, still pallid, still tremulous.

No woman with a woman's heart could have failed of pity or of sympathy; and two women, not of the hardest natures, were beside him there.

And Damian Aldenmede was watching them, seeing on the one face—the face he had turned to note first—a white, perturbed, pathetic sadness; on the other a burning and increasing sense of pain and anxiety, almost of fear; and yet it was easy to see that it was the fear that is waiting to be cast out by love. He could not but understand, at least up to a certain point; yet he knew that there was much behind that he could not see.

Half unknown to himself he was looking at this matter wholly through the eyes of another. However admirable Barbara Burdas might be as a woman of 'the masses,' strong to labour, yet with innate ideas of gentle living; having for duty's sake to give her life, her youth, her best energies to earning the bread of others as well as her own, yet cherishing a certain consciousness of the fact that man does not live by bread alone; content to spend the best of each day in toil that might even be considered disgusting; exposed to every element of an unkindly and hardening clime, yet indulging ceaseless yearnings after knowledge, after light, after good—yearnings that had to be kept in the straitest silence—however great, almost noble, all this in its way might be, Barbara was yet no fitting sister for the refined and cultured lady standing beside her now, making a contrast as complete as humanity could show.

All this and much more the artist saw; and in that moment it seemed to him that the truest kindness to Bab herself would be to endeavour to deliver her from the thraldom of the love into which she had so unwittingly fallen. He could see no happiness for her in any future that should include a union with this evidently hot-hearted, and perhaps more or less shallow-headed young man.

All unaware his mind was made up, and this with a swiftness, a want of deliberation almost unprecedented in his mental history. Later, he wondered over that hour by the sea at Ulvstan.

Not many seconds had passed since Hartas spoke. The young man was standing there, breathing quickly, glancing irately from one to another. As his glance fell upon Aldenmede the latter spoke:

'You were mentioning some errand, I think—some motive?' he began inquiringly, and in placid, respectful tones—the respect a man of good breeding instinctively displays to a stranger, however inferior that stranger may be to himself. All unknowingly poor Hartas was moved to a less antagonistic attitude for the moment.

'Yes; I did speak of an erran',' he said, his brown face coming to its natural brownness, with something over. 'I didn't risk my neck for nothing!'

'Naturally,' Aldenmede replied with unaffected gravity. He had seen that Miss Theyn was looking toward him pleadingly; that Bab's face was averted somewhat distressfully. 'Naturally you did not, and your motive must have been a tolerably strong one; and though I, perhaps, may have nothing to do with it....'

'I reckon you've more to do with it than you may be willin' to admit!' Hartas broke in angrily; 'an' if I were in your place I'd make no pretence o' not knowing.'

With a sudden gesture of impatience Bab turned herself towards the little group; a light flashed to her eyes—the light of remembrance. She had not seen the Squire's son except in the distance since that unhappy evening, when he had hurt her woman's sense of dignity by his too fervid and too hasty behaviour. For the moment his boldness, his rudeness, his roughness had caused a something that was almost revulsion in her heart. But naturally it was only, so to speak, for the moment, and it had been succeeded by a pathetic yearning for what she thought of in her own mind as a peace-making, or at any rate some understanding that should tend to a feeling of peace; and yet all the while she had precluded the possibility of any such opportunity happening to him; and this, though she knew that his yearning was at least as intense as her own. So it is ever with this

> 'Most illogical
> Irrational nature of our womanhood.
> That blushes one way, feels another way,
> And prays, perhaps, another.'*

And now again he was paining her, awakening within her a mingled sense of anger and heartache. Had she been alone with him, she had not shrunk from putting her pain into words, but as it was she could only restrain herself. Arresting the word that was on her lips, she turned away; but the artist had seen, and had in a measure understood.

There was yet no anger in Damian Aldenmede's heart; nothing but that large and generous pity.

'I am sorry if I have given you any cause of offence,' he said, speaking calmly. 'May I add that I have done so quite unconsciously?'

'All the same, you know what I mean?' asked Hartas.

'I fear I am beginning to suspect.'

* Mrs. Browning: *Aurora Leigh*.

'*I'll* put it into words for you,' said Barbara, coming forward and speaking tremulously. 'I'll help ya both if I can, since it seems to be me 'at's at the bottom o' the trouble. . . . Here's you' (turning to the artist), 'a stranger to the place, good an' kind-hearted, an' able to see when a woman's heart's aching for the need of help, of understandin', able *to see*, an' more nor that, willin' to give the help he knows to be needed; willin' to give time, an' trouble, an' pains to try to make that woman's life i' the present, and i' the future, seem brighter, an' pleasanter; better worth the livin'; willin' to give her, not only a word of encouragement, but to put the words into deeds; to come an' sit by the hour at a time in a little smoky fisherman's cottage, wi' the smell o' the oilskins, an' the salt fish, and the herrin's all about, an' never by no word nor sign to show no disgust, not for a moment; an' all this for the sake o' giving an hour's larnin' to one as had never had noän afore; but had gone on cravin' for help i' such things as a dumb beast out i' the cold might crave for the shelter it couldn't even pictur' to itself. . . . There! that's what *you* might say for yourself, if ya would. . . . An' as for you' (turning to Hartas Theyn, who stood near, with an air of uneasy sullenness), 'as for you, it's more difficult to say. You've thought to stoop down, to—to. . . .'

What ailed Barbara? What could ail a woman, young, strong, ignorant of nerves, of fainting, of hysteria? She had stopped suddenly: her breathing was coming and going rapidly, painfully; her whole frame seemed to be heaving with a sudden violence, and it was evident that no more words were possible to her. In trying to describe Hartas Theyn's position, had she attempted a task beyond her power; or was it merely that the emotion of the moment was too great to be borne?

No one had time to think.

Before Thorhilda could even attempt to comfort or soothe the girl, she perceived that two figures were rounding Yarva Ness; and almost at the same moment Barbara herself saw them. The Canon was helping Mrs. Godfrey over the slippery stones. Thorhilda went eagerly to meet them, with tearful face and outstretched hands. Here, at any rate, was strength and guidance.

'Come!' she exclaimed. 'Come and make peace, Uncle Hugh! Hartas is here—he came dashing right down the face of the cliff where it is steepest—he had seen Mr. Aldenmede sketching, and had taken some wrong notions into his head. Barbara Burdas was just telling him how wrong they were. Do come and put things right!'

It was very unusual to see Thorhilda so much excited, and her excitement caused the Canon to wonder how much the strength of any ordinary woman might be exhibited in her power to keep at least an outward show of calmness.

To Mrs. Godfrey, whose notions of propriety were, in a certain sense, rather rigid, it was somewhat annoying to have to be introduced to this stranger, of whom she had heard so much, under such circumstances as these. Nevertheless she smiled sweetly, and shook hands graciously, and did her best to hide her annoyance. Then she turned to Bab and Hartas, as she might have turned to two rather troublesome children in the Sunday-school, the beautiful smile still on her lip, a general expression of wondering amiability on her face.

'What is it all about, Hartas?' she asked; and anyone who had known Mrs. Godfrey well might, for all her amiable look, have detected a certain undertone of vexation. 'What is it? Ah! how I wish you would take my advice and leave Garlaff for awhile! It is unwise for a young man to remain always at home, unwise to give himself no chance of widening his mind, enlarging his experience, expanding his thoughts by contact with the thoughts and opinions of others. Do you not agree with me, Mr. Aldenmede?' she asked, turning quickly; but the artist was talking to her husband, Bab was listening to Thorhilda's pained regrets.

In the background, under the cliffs, half-a-dozen fishermen were crossing the beach, David Andoe among them, suddenly silenced in the middle of a story he had been repeating. He had recognised Bab from afar; he had seen that Hartas Theyn was one of the group; and now he was passing on, saddened, depressed with a depression that did not escape the notice of his mates. And for all the singularity they counted him to have, David was yet a favourite among them: and a whispered word was flashed along the little line of men like the lightning that goes before a storm. They understood, or believed that they did, and the new understanding added to the old determination; but the threat that Nan had heard was not repeated in David Andoe's hearing.

No one of the little group near the easel was dreaming of any ill to be. Mrs. Godfrey, as usual, equal to every occasion, was asking Mr. Aldenmede to dine at the Rectory on the following evening without ceremony. The Canon was talking to Hartas, sauntering on over the beach with him, drawing slowly from the youth a confession of a twofold jealousy, and therefore in all probability causeless on either hand. If Barbara were caring for David Andoe, she could certainly not be yielding to any fancy or feeling that might come of intercourse with such a man as Damian Aldenmede.

'You perplex me altogether,' the Canon said half-sadly, and trying to keep back all reproach from his tone. 'I can understand, believe me, I can understand more than you think of your unwise affection for Barbara Burdas; but it seems to me that if you truly cared for her, you would not run the risk of alienating her for ever by such displays of small jealousy as this! There is nothing small about Barbara. She will hardly endure behaviour of this kind; and I confess that you surprise me by apparently endeavouring to see how much she will bear. . . . Yet don't mistake me! I don't mean to be hard or unsympathetic; and I am sorry to see you suffering like this. But believe a man nearly twenty years older than yourself, and fifty years more experienced in the world's ways; believe me, when I say that you are not going the right way to work to win a large-hearted woman like Barbara Burdas. You are doing your utmost to repel her best and highest feeling. Perhaps I ought to be glad of this; but I cannot, quite honestly, say that I am.'

'Why not?' Hartas asked curtly, and with an evident disposition toward incredulousness.

'Why? . . . Well, shall I tell you the truth? Perhaps I had better! I am not glad, because I think I perceive that Barbara has some affection for you. If she have, it may save you! . . . There, you have all my reason!'

Slowly, half-unwillingly, and with a whole shyness, Hartas drew his clumsy brown hand from his pocket, and offered it to the Canon's grasp.

'I thank you for sayin' that,' the Squire's son replied. 'An' I trust you—that's more nor I can say for the most o' folks. . . . Yes, I trust *you*. . . . An' if I can help it, I'll go against you no more. I'll be different from to-day, if I can. I'd like to be different. I've wished it a good bit. Thorhilda told you mebbe.' (How strange it was that it should jar upon the Canon to hear his niece's Christian name used familiarly by her own brother.) 'She'd tell you 'at I'd been tryin' to make a change. But lately I've slipped back, an' I've been aware of it; but I couldn't help it, bein' so troubled; havin' no sort of hope nowhere. . . . But since you've told me *that*, I'll begin again. . . . I'll begin at once! I can't say no more!'

'I am glad you've said so much,' the Canon

replied, with an extreme quietude of voice and manner. 'And I am sure you mean it. I won't say any more now—only this: if you want help, help of any kind that I can give, will you come to me? I'll make things as easy for you as I can. . . . Promise me that you will come!'

'Ay, I'll promise that,' Hartas said, in tones that made Hugh Godfrey look up with an unintended quickness; he saw at once that the young fellow's eyes were suspiciously bright, as with tears held back by very force.

It was Hartas who delivered that last silent moment from its awkwardness.

'Good-day,' he said suddenly, again holding out his hand; 'I'll go back to Garlaff by way o' the Howes. It's none so far round from hereabouts.'

The Canon watched him a little as he went onward, sending after him a yearning look, a sigh, a prayer.

'There's plenty of good in the lad yet,' he said to himself, going back to the Ness. 'May God defend him from the powers of ill!'

## CHAPTER XXIV.

'SWEET THE HELP OF ONE WE HAVE HELPED.'

'Some men are nobly rich, *some nobly poor*,
Some the reverse.   Rank makes no difference.'
P. J. BAILEY : *Festus*.

DAMIAN ALDENMEDE had accepted the invitation of the Godfreys to dine at the Rectory.

'Come up to-morrow evening, if you can,' Mrs. Godfrey had said. 'There will only be ourselves, and perhaps Mr. Egerton ;' and the Canon had warmly seconded the invitation; adding, in his usual outspoken and simply cordial way :

'One does not too often, in a small place like Yarburgh, have the chance of a chat with congenially-minded people. I hope you are remaining some time ?'

'It will depend upon my work,' the artist had said ; and to Thorhilda's half-unconscious regret, the reply confirmed her impression of his dependence upon his own effort.

She could not help the sigh that came; but she might, by means of strong effort, have resisted the making of comparisons that should not have been made, with that tendency to concession growing daily in her heart which Percival Meredith was daily expecting; always waiting for it with a finely diplomatic patience. There should be no haste; and, until the right moment came, no more pressure.

Owing to the seclusion in which he lived, Damian Aldenmede had heard nothing of Miss Theyn's supposed engagement; though everywhere the matter was now spoken of as if no doubt existed. The artist was not a man to whom people could gossip; even his landlady was learning this, somewhat to her perplexity.

All day—that is, all his working day—he had been painting in Yarva Wyke. Bab and Ailsie had been sitting to him for about an hour; but Bab's mind had been too full of a recent event to permit of her being quite so perfect a model as she usually was.

The story was soon told. In the night a screw-steamer had cut her way through the herring-nets belonging to the *Star of the North*. There had been lights on board the fishing-boat; every reasonable and usual precaution had been attended to, yet disaster had overtaken the poor fishermen in the hour of their midnight toil.

'It means many a bright pound to us,' Bab admitted, when at last the artist's evident sympathy unloosed her tongue; though even then she regretted the confession; and added, 'of course, we share it among us. There's five of us—we'll get over it somehow.'

The artist hesitated a while, trying first to find the exact thought he wanted, then the word. It was not easy to find the latter on the spur of the moment.

By way of temporising, he said, 'Is the name of the steamer known?'

'Yes, they saw it on her stern fair enough as she sheered off. She was the *Oriana*, of Cardiff.'

'And can no redress be had—I mean, cannot an action be brought to compel the owners of the vessel to pay at least something toward the damage done to the nets?'

Bab laughed, a sad, sarcastic, understanding little laugh.

'It is little you know,' she replied, not meaning to be unflattering. 'Why there's never a week i' the herring season but somebody's nets is cut all to bits. An' where d'ya think fisher-folks 'ud get the money to go to law, wi' the lawyers all on the side o' the rich owners? It 'ud cost more to pay the law bills than you could get new nets for. No, we never think o' seekin' justice. The law isn't for such as us; an' the owners an' captains o' them screw-steamers know it. They'd be more careful if they'd any fear.'

Again the artist was silent for a moment. Presently, speaking with a grave considerateness, he said:

"It seems to me then that there is only one earthly hope for you—the help of friends. For instance, since you have helped me so much—you and Ailsie, given me such help that in all probability my picture will be hung in the Grosvenor Gallery—that is a place in

London where many beautiful pictures are hung, and sometimes sold—since you have given me this help, why should I not help you? Why should I not provide your grandfather's boat, or rather the one he has a share in, with new nets? ... I should like to do it! Will you allow me?'

Barbara's face as she listened was certainly a study; and one worthy of any portrait-painter's best attention. The sadness that was half-amusement, the wonder that was half-pity, would have taxed any ordinary talent to the uttermost.

'You'll buy new nets for the *Star o' the North?*' she said, with an inquiring note in her accent not quite free from something that was almost derision. 'What d'ya suppose they'd cost? Ninepence a-piece, mebbe? or it may be you'd think of hevin' to go as far as eighteenpence! Eh, me! Why, *a new set complete 'ud never cost far short of a hundred pounds!* Think o' that! An' you to talk o' *givin'* 'em, as one 'ud give a tramp 'at asked for a light for his pipe a farden box o' matches! Eh, but you mun know little o' the valley o' money if that's how you think on it! New nets for a fishin' coble! It fair stuns one to hear ya talk!'

The artist had listened quite gravely, subdued his amusement to interest quite successfully.

'A hundred pounds, did you say?'

'Ay! That's what I said! . . . Anyhow, buyin' the nets at the very cheapest we'll never get 'em for no less nor ninety.'

'That is a large sum, relatively,' the artist replied. . . . 'But—I do not tell you this by way of boasting; quite the reverse—last year I sold a picture for about the same price. It was one that I had painted in a very short time, and happening to have no need of the money, I have not touched it. . I had reasons for wishing not to put it to any of the ordinary uses of life. For one thing, it was the first picture I had ever sold; for another' (and here the artist hesitated, and seemed embarrassed), 'for another reason, something had passed between the buyer of the picture and myself long ago, very long ago, that made me wish to put the money aside for some especial purpose, some emergency happening to some life—not my own. It seems to me that this emergency is now before me. I could buy the nets; and so far from missing the money, I should feel that I had, at last, freed myself from a trust.'

The look of wonder, of perplexity, was deepening on Barbara's face; sadness and wistfulness mingling with it.

'There's a lot o' things you could buy for a hundred pounds!' she said presently.

'True! I have told you why I cannot buy them, with that money. Though, please remember, I told you in confidence. Perhaps I do not need to add that.'

Barbara looked into his eyes steadfastly.

'If I thought you mistrusted me once, you'd have no opportunity o' doin' it again,' she said, adding, 'Eh, but it does take folks a long time to know one another down to the bottom!'

There was another brief silence before she spoke again. Evidently she had been thinking of the artist rather than of herself.

'If ya couldn't buy nought wi' that money, ya might live in better lodgin's. Yon's none a place for you!'

'Why not? But, if it troubles you, I may

say that I could, if I wished to do so, stay at the hotel. It is not on account of the expense that I prefer the Forecliff.'

'At the "Empress o' India," Bab said, rather to herself than quite aloud. It was only the other day that Mrs. Nossifer at the fish-shop in the Cliff Road at Yarburgh had told her that the gentlemen who stayed at the new hotel at Ulvstan were charged a guinea a day for their food and lodging. Bab had accepted the fact as surprising, but not as one likely ever to concern herself, or even anyone she might know. Now she recalled it in silence.

'You have not given me any answer?' the artist said presently, in a tone of inquiry. 'Tell me what you are thinking.'

'I'm thinking this,' Bab replied with a quite new emphasis, and tremulously conscious of a certain amount of daring. 'I'm thinkin' 'at you're noän what you seem. . . . You're noän one o' them 'at paints pictures for a livin'.'

'No? What makes you think that?'

'Everything! You've none the manner, nor the bearin' o' them 'at hes to depend on other folk for the bread they eat.'

Aldenmede paused a moment; then he said:

'Granted, so far! For if I am not working solely for my own bread, why should I not try to help those who must do so? why, for instance, should you refuse to allow me to help you in a trouble that has unexpectedly come upon you?'

Barbara looked at him again; her lips were trembling with the unsaid words, but her thought was not for herself, nor wholly of the artist. She had others in her mind, others to whom this munificence would seem as a miraculous gift of God.

'You may help if you will,' she said at last. The words might have been counted ungracious, but her manner, the emotion of it, neutralized all idea of that kind. 'You may if you will,' she repeated. Then, out of the fulness of her heart, rather than by aid of any shadow of impertinence, she added, 'I'd noän be surprised if ya turned out to be a duke.'

Much laughter was not in Aldenmede's way, yet to his relief and to Bab's he indulged for once. Presently, still smiling, he said:

'I suppose, then, that all the surprise would be on my part! Certainly it would be very great. .... Believe me, your imagination is running away with you!'

'But noän sa far?'

'Very far indeed.'

'You've no title o' no sort?'

'Not a shadow of one. I should like, I should very much like to write R.A. after my name, or even A.R.A., which means something much less. But I am talking idly. Enough of pleasantries of that kind. They are not so very pleasant after all. .... And now it is all settled! I may buy the nets?'

'Will ya think on it till the mornin'?'

'No; pardon me, I have given more than enough of thought to the matter. I have other things to think of.'

'Yes; so you have,' Barbara replied after a moment of hesitation. 'Things 'at's mebbe even more to you nor that.' ... Then, with a swift change of tone, she said, 'You're goin' up there to get your dinner to-night—to the Rectory?'

'Yes.'

'Do you like goin'?'

'Yes. I am very glad to go.'

'I don't doubt it. . . . . Yet I'm noän envyin' you.'

'No. I should not think that a common enviousness was much in your way.'

'You can see that? . . . Well, it's true. Still, one can't help thinkin' sometimes; sometimes wishin'. . . . Why is there such difference atween one an' another?'

'Why, indeed?'

The fisher-girl had set a problem that the educated gentleman was almost as unable to solve as she herself was, though he was not thinking about it now for the first time. Yet, seeing that the question had been asked in no bitterness of heart or mood, he did his best to make the girl perceive up to the point he himself perceived.

'*Why* these differences between class and class exist is more than I can say,' he answered. 'Perhaps it is more than anyone can say. It is enough for a reverent mind that they were ordained of God. Along the whole line of what we term sacred history there is proof of that from the day when we hear of the herdsmen who tended Abram's cattle to this day. But there is proof also that God Himself had a special regard for the poor. David perceived that; and the mere fact of God's own Son *choosing* a life of poverty should reconcile some of us who are very far from any true reconciliation. Still, it is a mystery. One might think, to read of the pauperism, the suffering of the poor of our own time, that God had forgotten them, or had, at least, forgotten to be gracious; but that can never be. *Why* He permits such suffering I cannot tell; but this I can tell, that it is the duty of everyone who is *not* suffering to do something for those who are; to think of them and for them; to try at least to comfort them in their sorrows; to help them over their troubles; in a word, to show them some friendliness, some human loving-kindness.'

'It's the poor 'at helps the poor, for the most part,' said Bab, speaking almost like one in a dream. 'I could tell ya many a tale o' things 'at's happened at Ulvstan Bight, things 'at might surprise ya. It was yesterday ya were speaking o' self-sacrifice, an' I thought o' some I know. We're noän such a hard lot as you might think!'

'You shall tell me some of the tales before I go away; that is if you will.'

'Before you go away! .... You're noän goin'!'

The artist smiled not unpleasantly.

'You did not think I had come to live in Ulvstan Bight, did you?'

'Mebbe not,' Bab replied. Then more wistfully she asked, 'But ya'll noän go till the picture's done, will ya?'

'I shall not need to stay here to finish it. .... But I can do no more to-day. .... Will you ask your grandfather to come and have a chat with me to-morrow morning? I want to know more about those accidents to the fishing-nets.'

# CHAPTER XXV.

DAMIAN ALDENMEDE AT THE RECTORY.

'Have you seen but a bright lily grow
    Before rude hands have touched it?
Have you marked but the fall of the snow
    Before the soil has smutched it?
Have you felt the wool of the beaver?
    Or swan's-down ever?
Or have smelt o' the bud of the briar?
    Or the nard in the fire?
Or have tasted the bag o' the bee?
Oh, so white! oh, so soft! oh so sweet is she!'
                      BEN JONSON.

IT is strange how some men seem to change with the changing of the society about them; there might even seem to be hypocrisy in such modifications, or at least weakness of will and character. But in truth these drawbacks are not always existent. A sensitive nature responds to its environment so unconsciously that it is often utterly unaware of its own facility in responding, and the too-friendly friend who shall point out the seeming inconsistency may give a thrust not lightly or easily borne.

You are in trouble, or you have pain, apprehension, and you write a letter to an old friend who has known your history from first to last. Naturally, almost inevitably, you permit yourself the relief of an utter outpouring. You may know yourself to be even morbidly apprehensive, yet you dare to admit this; you are aware that you are feeling some pain, mental and physical, with an undue keenness; yet you can confess it, and this readily, gladly. Or some little bit of unusual joy has come in your way, and in unwonted exuberance of spirit you ask that your friend shall rejoice with you. In a word, you wear your heart, not on your sleeve, but on a sheet or two of note-paper. And, believe it always, the true friend is drawn to be truer; he would scorn to betray you to even his own soul's censure.

That letter written, you write another to another correspondent, you date it with the same date, write it in the same hour; yet this second letter shall be (without your being wholly aware of it) stiff and chill and pallid. Not only heart shall be missing, but soul, spirit, even intellect.

Were these letters read out to you on a later day, in the presence, not of enemies (we none of us have enemies in these suave times), but of friends who are on sufficiently intimate terms with you to express the measure of their friendliness by the amount of their freedom, you would blush for your own apparent duplicity. It would seem nothing less than that.

And yet there is no equivocation, no intentional or other insincerity. A man's nature is manifold, and can turn this side to the friend who wins his confidence, this to the man whose talent he admires, this to one who needs only a social courtesy; so it is that he can meet so many other human souls with some human pleasure, some refreshment. It is only the narrow of spirit, the uncultured in social intercourse, who imagine that they discern mendacity in this varied face turned to a varying humanity.

Naturally enough Damian Aldenmede was unaware that he was a different man to his host and hostess at the Rectory from that he had seemed to be to Barbara Burdas. To the latter he was genial, sympathetic, not caring to hide the fact that he was thoughtful for her present and her future. To the former he was a grave and comparatively silent man—in a certain sense evidently a man of the world, betraying a distinction of manner and aspect that instantly won its due regard. And yet the Godfreys, as well as their niece, were conscious of something to which they could put no name. To have used the word 'mystery' would have been to suggest something that none of them for a moment intended.

He did not talk much of himself, this new guest, and no one at the Rectory, save Gertrude Douglas, made the slightest attempt to induce him to do so. And though it could not be said that he declined to respond to her effort, yet but little real knowledge was elicited. He was an Englishman, he had travelled much abroad, especially in Italy, and had been glad to return to his own country. He gave a decided impression of having nothing to hide; but, on the other hand, he made it evident that he did not greatly care to permit himself to become a topic of conversation in his own presence. His host took care that his desire was respected.

The dinner passed off as dinners at the Rectory always did, pleasantly and easily. No display for display's sake was visible; no neglect or inadequacy tolerated. The Canon was in one of his happiest and most winning moods. Mr. Egerton was, as usual, equal to anything and everything that came in his way; and the conversation sparkled about this topic and about that, as it will when people give themselves, for the lighter social hour, to interchange of the more superficial ideas of life and living. But gradually, almost inevitably, the stream deepened. Before the evening was over the new guest was better comprehended at Yarburgh Rectory.

It was evident that he had intended no betrayal of himself. All unaware he was drawn by the Canon's earnestness to confess his own; perhaps confessing more than he was well aware of.

'You say that it is weighing upon you more than anything else — the present condition of the poor of England, of your own parish,' he had replied in answer to a remark the Canon had made. 'I can well believe it. I have often thought that it must be even more terrible for a clergyman than for anyone else.'

'So it is; he stands in such a different position toward the poor. He preaches a gospel of brotherhood, or professes to do so; but mostly he refrains from details on that head in his sermons; and perhaps wisely. For what does such brotherhood mean, for even the best of us? What do we really know of our brother? What do we really care? In the heart of us, what is the depth of our caring?'

'Be moderate!' interrupted Mr. Egerton, his *spirituel* face lighting up with earnest entreaty. 'Don't run the risk of giving a false impression. Mr. Aldenmede is a stranger; he may take you at your own valuation!'

'It would be wise of him to do so. Mr. Aldenmede has seen enough, known enough of humanity, to know that no man confesses himself a sinner who has not sinned; not unless he has tendencies more or less morbid, an accusation of which I am not afraid.'

'Doesn't it rather depend upon what one calls sin, or even error, or mistake?' the artist asked. 'With regard to the problem of the suffering poor we have all of us erred, most of us are yet erring; but one is glad to see everywhere a certain sensitiveness on the subject, oft enough showing itself in irritation, annoyance, sometimes in incredulousness, sometimes in an attempt to prove that each state of life has its own "compensations." What can be the compensation for having no fire, no food, no clothing worth the name; no decent bed even; and only the most inhuman shelter?'

'But,' said Mr. Egerton, 'but short of that extreme of want, putting all such extremes aside for the moment, do you not think that even the life of the very poor has alleviations?'

'Alleviations!' exclaimed Aldenmede. 'Yes, thank Heaven! One is glad to know that it has, to believe in it to the uttermost. I may say that some of the happiest and pleasantest people I have known have been people who were living from week to week. Alleviation! Their life is, in many cases, full of it! So long as things keep on at the moderate level of possible living they have few cares, anxiety dies down, fear for the future is quiescent. Such people often have the kindliest feelings; they have known trouble, sickness, loss, pain; and these things have made them sympathetic, and sympathy brings them nearer to their friends and neighbours. Oh, "love in a cottage" is not a dream! It may be an ideal; but it might be the most magnificent, most beneficent ideal. It wants raising, however. The man who lives and loves in a cottage wants help for the most part, such help as can only come from those who are somewhat his superiors in culture, in insight. He wants teaching *how* to find delight in books, in music, in art, in all things lovely, and pure, and of good report; the things that elevate thought, that awaken the beginnings of aspiration. He needs to be made to perceive that the mere possession of houses, of land, of capital, can do nothing to help his highest happiness; to be shown how, in the simplest wayside cottage, life may be lived as its very best, life intellectual, life spiritual —nay, one might almost say the perfect life which has been the ideal of the saints from the first Christian century to this nineteenth. It has never died out, the grand vision. It never can. Perfection! Well for the man who has not ceased to dream of it, to yearn for it, to work for it! If the mere yearning exists in any man, that man is to be envied. How to implant it where it does not exist should be one of the problems of the modern philanthropist.'

Thorhilda had been seated at the piano for the last half-hour, now and then playing one of the softer of Mendelssohn's Lieder, now and then stopping to listen, to say a few words to Gertrude Douglas, who was sitting with her embroidery near the table by the piano. It was evident that the evening was proving more or less a disappointing one to Miss Douglas; and Thorhilda, seeing that such was the case, left the piano and went to the fireside, where her uncle stood on the rug, the new guest near him.

Mrs. Godfrey was seated on the sofa by the fire.

'Are you not tired of my uncle's parochial conversation?' Miss Theyn asked, looking into Mr. Aldenmede's sad, grave face. 'Uncle Hugh, I know, will never be tired; but he may weary other people. . . . I often wish I were poor—quite poor, like Barbara Burdas, for instance; then he would care for me!'

There was a pause. The artist was watching the piquant humour of the lovely face before him, the changing light in the gray appealing eyes, the tender winning smile with which she turned to her uncle. What sweetness such a woman was capable of putting into any home-life! What beauty! What grace! Even for one evening to taste of such life, to feel the warmth of it, was like coming under some touch of enchantment.

The artist had forgotten the reply he intended to make. 'Barbara Burdas!' he said at last. 'What a good woman she is! Speaking of the poor, of their desert, their endurance, where will you find a braver or a better girl? Think of all that she has done, is yet doing, and by her own unaided strength, so far as human help is concerned! She likes to keep up the fiction that her grandfather helps; and naturally the old man likes to keep up the same comforting notion. But it is a notion utterly mistaken. She profits somewhat by his share, or part of a share, in the *Star of the North*, but last year the sum was less than four pounds; it did not pay for the rent of the house. And this year, owing to accidents, damage done by the trawlers, and suchlike things, she is afraid it will be even less; yet she never utters a word of complaint. It is old Ephraim who does the complaining, though he admits that he " wants for nothing." '

'The most striking thing about Barbara is her craving for knowledge, for education, said the Canon, who knew a little of what was being said in the Bight as to the artist's kindness in lending the girl books, helping her to understand them, and teaching her in a general way something of the right use and meaning of her own language. But the Canon made no direct reference to the subject, though he perceived that Miss Douglas was waiting with suspended needle for details of the matter.

She was not to be gratified. Aldenmede replied only to what the Canon had said.

'That is one striking thing; another is her hatred of all coarseness or roughness, her desire for refinement; and being surrounded by things rough and coarse, her duty seeming to lie amongst them, her everyday life must be more or less one of pain to a sensitive nature. Yet I do not believe that she ever dreams of escape of any kind; that in one sense she can even be said to desire it. That is the touchstone. She does her duty, and more; and being urged onward and upward by unseen influences she knows no content in so doing. How should she? Contentment is not for such as Barbara. To be content is too often to know no aspiration for one's self or for others, to know no sympathy, to have no human outlook, no passionate human desire for progress, for attainment of any kind. Contentment! It is for the cattle in the fields, that graze and fatten and die! No thinking human soul can in these days be contented.'

Thorhilda was listening, thinking, recalling the speech of another on the same topic, and as she thought her heart-beats came the faster. Was she not deliberately dreaming of this lower content? And at what cost? Never had the price seemed to be what it seemed now with this stranger standing by her uncle's hearth, unveiling his own heart, his own aspiration, all unknowingly. She shrank even from herself as she listened. It was as if some voice were heard drawing her from ease, from wealth, from luxury, entreating her to take some higher way. And, harder still, this higher way was made attractive. She could hardly help fearing that this stranger had read her true character. She seemed to discern his perception in every look, every word. And the more she discerned, the more she was drawn to watch for further signs. Here, if anywhere, was the guide she had longed for, the one true helper, the one adequate friend. Again the feeling that she had first known on that day by the sea came back to her, but with redoubled emotion, and again it was followed by the remembrance that all such feelings must be put strongly away.

'Strongly and surely,' she said to herself that night in her own room as she walked up and down, trying to quiet her unsettled spirit, yet unable to put away from her mental vision that grave yet tender glance, to close her ears to the tones of the most sympathetic, and sad, and kindly voice she had ever heard. Now, for the first time, she realized what it was to be subjugated by a look, coerced by a turn of the head, silenced by another's silence. What might it mean, this new and peculiar experience? Whatever it meant it must be put away, and the sooner the better, the better for everyone concerned. 'It is evident he does not know,' Thorhilda continued to herself, 'he has not heard of—of Mr. Meredith, of his friendship for me. He must know soon, very soon! Then it will be over—this—this unrest, this strain. It will all be over, and I shall be at peace. . . . Will he come again? It would be better that he should not—better far. . . . Yet it would be pleasant, very pleasant. . . . And I am not a fool. . . . Indeed, now that I think of it, I should *wish* him to come to the Rectory again, that I might prove to myself my self-possession. I wish it, certainly I do, and I wish that he may come soon! The sooner he comes the sooner will this unrest be ended.'


END OF VOL. I.

www.ingramcontent.com/pod-product-compliance
Lightning Source LLC
Chambersburg PA
CBHW032055220426
43664CB00008B/1009